MASTERING MONERO

The future of private transactions

SerHack and the Monero Community

Credits

Content
- 4matter
- Amichateur
- Anonimal
- ArticMine
- Cryptochangements
- dEBRUYNE
- Isthmus
- Midipoet
- moneroexamples
- QuickBASIC
- Rehrar
- Sarang Noether
- Xeagu

Designers
- Gustaf Baltsar Garnow
- TheMonera

Illustrator
- Andrés Fernández Cordón

Publisher
- Justin Ehrenhofer

Editor
- UncagedPotential

Mastering Monero is made available as a free digital resource through the generosity of Monero FFS donors. The author and community have invested over 2100 hours into crafting this book as a helpful guide for both novice and experienced Monero users. We hope that you find this reference to be valuable and share it widely.

Published by LernoLibro LLC.

First edition: December 2018

Mastering Monero is an extensive community effort, and such lengthy resources are likely to contain mistake(s).

If you find any technical issues or grammatical/spelling mistakes, please report your finding to:
support@masteringmonero.com

Table of Content

Writing Mastering Monero

About the author

I am Nico ("SerHack"), an Italian security researcher, a Monero contributor, and the author of this book. Finding good resources and learning about cryptocurrencies can be a daunting task. For new users, it can be especially challenging to track down documentation written at an understandable technical level. When I first started learning about Monero, I had to spend a great deal of time seeking out and evaluating many different resources on the topic.

I decided to write *Mastering Monero* to guide you along this journey, whether you're setting up your first wallet or curious about the 'under the hood' technical details. The first few chapters are written for anybody curious about why and how to use Monero; they contain easy-to-understand explanations and examples, alongside instructions for practical use. Later chapters progress into more advanced topics, compiling information for developers who wish to build and contribute to the Monero ecosystem.

My adventure into the world of cryptocurrencies began when I learned about Bitcoin in January 2016, and I was always concerned about the ramifications of its transparent public ledger. Since Bitcoin and most other cryptocurrencies are built around openly-linked addresses and coins with clear histories, transactions often inadvertently expose users' personal financial details. Every address balance is public information, which allows anybody to research income, spending habits, and amount of cryptocurrency wealth. This can lead to undesirable consequences, such as price manipulation based on wallet balance.

I thought that Bitcoin was the only cryptocurrency until a friend introduced me to Monero in May 2017. I was blown away by its beautiful new paradigm: a world where vulnerable details such as account balances and transaction amounts are kept confidential to protect both the sender and the receiver. With privacy features implemented by default and always required, the entire Monero blockchain is veiled; users do not even have the option to accidentally send revealing transactions.

Recognizing the importance of this project, I began looking for ways to contribute to the community. I quickly saw an opportunity to support mass adoption by building payment gateways for online businesses, so I spearheaded the Monero Integrations project. This open-source codebase is designed around Monero's privacy-centric mentality: no signup or third-party service is required, since funds are routed directly to the recipient's wallet. The Monero community was very supportive throughout this endeavor, and the entire project was crowdfunded by donations through the Monero Forum Funding System (FFS).

While working on the Monero Integrations project, I learned that the lack of a comprehensive guide to Monero was an obstacle for end users and prospective contributors. This need for a thorough guide inspired me to write *Mastering Monero* as a universal resource for our global community. I am grateful for the generous FFS support that has made it possible to publish this document as a free eBook (and physical book!) for the general public. Whether you read *Mastering Monero* cover-to-cover or jump through sections pertinent to your questions, I hope you enjoy learning about Monero and the exciting projects within the community.

How this resource is organized

The first two chapters of this book are friendly non-technical introductions to key topics and skills. For readers curious to learn more about behind-the-scenes details, chapters 3 and 4 contain conceptual non-mathematical explanations of Monero's privacy features and blockchain. Later chapters dive into complex technical details for understanding, developing, and integrating Monero.

The first chapter (*Introduction to cryptocurrencies & Monero*) is an general-audience non-technical introduction covering key ideas and concepts about blockchains and cryptocurrencies (appropriate both for newcomers and current users wishing to read more about Monero's principles). We'll cover the history and basics of cryptocurrencies, and describe how using blockchain technology resolves several problems present in the traditional mainstream financial systems, especially banking services. Unfortunately, there are privacy weaknesses endemic to most cryptocurrencies - we'll discuss the personal implications of these drawbacks, and learn how Monero mitigates these risks and protects your sensitive financial information.

The second chapter (*Getting started: receiving, storing and sending Monero*) is your handy guide for all the practical skills and tools that you'll need to use Monero yourself! We'll explain some necessary lingo, and learn about the 'pros and cons' of types of wallets. You'll learn how to make your first wallet, and you can even use the Mastering Monero example wallet for practice!

In the third chapter (*How Monero works*), we'll discuss Monero's four main privacy technologies: RingCT, ring signatures, one-time (stealth) addresses, and Kovri. These are friendly explanations with no use of math or code, so you can learn conceptually how each feature works, and what benefits they provide.

The fourth chapter (*The Monero Network*) conceptually describes how Monero's network and miners processes transactions onto the blockchain. We'll discuss miners' incentivization (block rewards + fees), and the services that miners provide (confirming transaction and securing the decentralized and trustless network). We'll also introduce the "hot topic" of specialized mining equipment, and describe the Monero community's relevant egalitarian philosophy and active countermeasures that have been taken to resist ASICs.

While the preceding chapters have focused on learning how to use and conceptualize Monero in practical and intuitive ways. The remainder of the book will dive deeply into the internals of Monero, its mathematics, and its code. If you choose to tackle these advanced topics, you will truly be "mastering" Monero!

The fifth chapter (*A Deep Dive into Monero & Cryptography*) leads a technical deep dive into the privacy technologies covered conceptually in chapter 3. This study moves pass the analogies, into the actual mathematics and specifications of Monero's enhanced version of the CryptoNote protocol.

The sixth chapter (*Community and Contributing*) contains information for anybody that is interested in contributing their time and skills to help the Monero community. Whatever your strengths, there are opportunities to contribute - you could help with translations, outreach, code development, applications, or in many other ways.

The seventh chapter (*Monero integration for developers*) discusses payment option, and useful methods for conveying addresses through OpenAlias (human-readable) and the Monero URI (machine-readable). Developers for merchant payment options, learn about generating simplified addresses through OpenAlias. Developers will learn how to interact with the Monero blockchain via remote procedure calls (RPC) to the Monero daemon, and a Python implementation is included to teach how basic tasks are executed.

The eighth chapter (*Wallet guide and troubleshooting tips*) contains miscellaneous information for setting up a graphical (GUI) or terminal-based (CLI) wallet along with troubleshooting tips for common problems.

## Chapter 1

Introduction to cryptocurrencies & Monero

Maria is purchasing a car from George, and in this chapter we'll consider three different ways that she could pay him: traditional banks, transparent cryptocurrencies (e.g. Bitcoin), and Monero.

1.1 Payment through banks

Figure 1.1 - Maria sends money to George through the traditional banking system.

If Maria sends the money to George through the traditional banking system, they trust two intermediate parties (their respective banks) to symbolically move the funds for them.

There is no actual movement of physical bills or assets; both banks simply edit their respective databases to show that the funds have been transferred. When Maria submits the transaction to her bank (whether by wire transfer, her bank's website, or an app), her bank subtracts $2,500 from her account balance on their ledger, then contacts George's bank and requests that they add $2,500 to George's balance.

There are a few drawbacks and risks to this system, and it requires total trust in the banks. Maria, George, and the banks must act on faith that transactions are legitimate and that the ledgers are kept honestly. This trust in the intermediate third parties poses a risk, since a nefarious actor or the banks could "create" money by fraudulently editing the ledger balances or transaction database.

Furthermore, Maria does not actually have possession of $3900, only an IOU from her bank that she must trust is redeemable. She has no way to audit her bank to verify whether they actually have $3900.

In fact, they may not hold that much, since most banks legally operate on *fractional reserve* - meaning that their actual assets are allowed to be significantly less than the total balance promised to account owners.

Depending on how the funds were sent, it could take anywhere from minutes to days before the $2,500 shows up in George's bank account. Since George is not privy to the banks' ledgers or communications, the entire process is opaque and cannot be monitored.

Many people that have not personally experienced economic disruption take functioning banks and the validity of their IOUs for granted. Few individuals consider the unsettling ramifications of handing their lifelong savings to opaque corporations, often putting all their eggs in a single institutional basket. Losses can occur due to:

- negligence (the bank makes a mistake)

- financial issues (the bank overextends their assets or goes out of business)

- malice and corruption (the bank or a rogue employee steals your money)

- hostile third parties (the bank is robbed or a hacker thieves electronic funds)

Thankfully, an emerging new blockchain technology is capable of mitigating all of the above risks by creating a distributed ledger that all parties can equally use, view, and verify. This remarkable capability for strangers to agree on a shared document, which is called decentralized consensus, has been revolutionized in the last decade.

It's easy to be confused about the terminology at first, especially since most people are simultaneously introduced to several jargony concepts. You can think about "blockchains" as a *technology* that allows networks to establish "decentralized consensus" agreements. By enabling strangers to safely share a ledger, it becomes possible to build "cryptocurrencies" that function as digital cash. There are a multitude of regular currencies (euros, dollars, yen, etc); analogously, various teams have built many different cryptocurrencies (Monero, Ethereum, Bitcoin, etc).

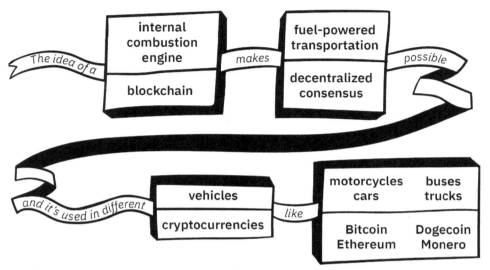

Figure 1.2 - An analogy showing parallels between various cryptocurrency terms (blockchain, decentralized consensus, and cryptocurrencies) and words related to common transportation.

1.2 Introduction to blockchains

Anybody can learn all about Monero and how its blockchain works without having to understand the underlying mathematics and cryptography (similar to how anybody can become internet-savvy without first studying DNS servers and the IPv6 protocol). **This chapter focuses on the key concepts and vocabulary without digging into all of the technical details** - you can jump ahead to chapter 4 and chapter 5 if you want to dive into the cryptographic framework.

1.2.1 What is a blockchain?

The term *blockchain* refers to a particular method for securing records in a database that all network users share. It is groundbreaking for being a *trustless* system, where individuals retain full autonomy over their funds, there is no central authority, and each participant can easily verify and audit the system.

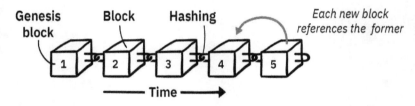

Figure 1.3 - Every few minutes, the network adds another permanent block of information onto the chain, securely linked to the previous block by its hash.

Anyone in the world is welcome to act as a network maintainer, and each participant keeps the others honest by verifying the blockchain. When users broadcast information to be placed on the blockchain, network maintainers group these transmissions into *blocks* and use cryptographic tools to finalize the records and permanently link them onto the blockchain.

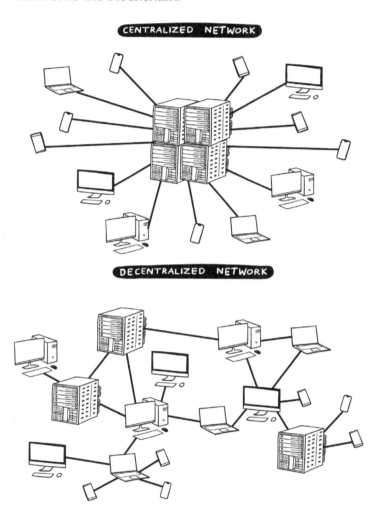

Figure 1.4 - In a traditional centralized network (top) all of the users must connect to designated machines maintained by a third party, shown by the central hub of server racks. In a decentralized network (bottom) the users created an ad-hoc web of interconnected machines. Monero uses this latter type of system with no special centralized servers, instead employing a resilient peer-to-peer network of volunteer nodes sharing new information with each other.

Once data is sealed onto the blockchain, it cannot be deleted, moved, or altered in any way. The records are immutable and each participant on the network has matching copy of the blockchain for their own verification. Most cryptocurrency blockchains employ a clever *mining* model that encourages network participation and keeps all of the records honest and synchronized. These types of *decentralized* systems are incredibly robust since there is no single server or central database that can be maliciously attacked or manipulated.

These decentralized systems are also *trustless* since each participant in the network maintains and verifies their own copy of the records, instead of relying on any third party. Given that blockchains provide a system for global tamperproof recordkeeping, they are extremely well-suited for storing financial data. In fact, the first modern distributed blockchain debuted in 2008 as the mechanism underlying the Bitcoin cryptocurrency.

On October 31st 2008, an anonymous individual or group known as Satoshi Nakamoto published a whitepaper describing *"Bitcoin: A Peer-to-Peer Electronic Cash System."* This world-changing document laid out the framework for the open-source decentralized crypto-currency and the revolutionary blockchain technology that makes it possible.

Figure 1.1 in the first section highlighted how sending money through the traditional banking system requires multiple transactions, separate ledgers, and trust in more than one bank. **Figure 1.5** (below) shows how Maria could send money to George by transferring 10.5 Bitcoin from her address (1BuUygisXY) to an address controlled by George (1eK5FSywkp). This example references Bitcoin (BTC) for convenience, however nearly **all** cryptocurrencies use this type of public ledger and thus experience the following benefits and issues.

Figure 1.5 - Maria sends money to George using a cryptocurrency with a transparent public blockchain, such as Bitcoin.

1.2.2 Blockchain benefits

A few of the blockchain benefits are immediately apparent:

- **Simplicity (& speed)**: Maria's money is broadcast to George in a single step to update a single ledger. Whereas bank and wire transfers can take days or weeks, cryptocurrency ledgers typically update in seconds or minutes (the transaction confirmation time varies for different cryptocurrencies).

- **No third-party risks**: Maria and George rely on their own cryptographically-secured and self-maintained system instead of placing their money and trust in the hands of third parties.

- **Pseudo-anonymity**: Unlike the banks, cryptocurrency ledgers never record real names such as "Maria" and "George" with the accounts. In fact, personal information is never necessary for generating an cryptocurrency wallet. George will access the funds pseudonymously, using his key for the `1eK5FSywkp` address to which Maria broadcasted the money (from her account, `1BuUygisXY`).

Bitcoin and the other cryptocurrencies that followed have initiated a financial revolution that is still unfolding. With these new decentralized networks, anybody can personally store and globally transfer funds at their own discretion. Prior to cryptocurrencies, it was difficult to store large amounts of wealth securely without trusting your savings to banks or credit unions. Likewise, transferring money to another individual or business required reliance on third-party payment processors for checks, wire transfers, or credit/debit cards.

Thanks to cryptocurrencies, for the first time, anybody can exercise their basic financial rights without requiring access to a bank and approval from external institutions! In mere moments, any device (computer, phone, tablet) can be used to initialize a new cryptocurrency wallet that is fully functional for receiving, storing, and sending funds. Setting up a wallet does not require any kind of identification, fees, or authorization, since the system identifies users by addresses that look like random strings of numbers and letters instead of personally identifiable details such as names, street addresses, or phone numbers.

1.2.3 Blockchain drawbacks

Most cryptocurrencies are *pseudo-anonymous*, since their users are identified by unintelligible strings of letters and numbers rather than personal identifiers. When you receive a cryptocurrency payment, you do not learn the sender's name; instead, you receive the funds from an address such as: `1A1zP1eP5QGefi2DMPTfTL5SLmv7DivfNa`.

While this preserves privacy in some ways, it also exposes some sensitive information. Recall, every participant in a decentralized blockchain system can access a complete copy of the entire set of records. In the context of cryptocurrencies, this ledger is used to ascertain the account balance for any (e.g. Bitcoin) address.

On these shared transparent ledgers every account balance and history is public! In fact, several helpful websites allow you to easily search the blockchain for any address or transaction.

Suppose you run a shop, and one of your customers pays for a loaf of bread from the Bitcoin address `3P3QsMVK89JBNqZQv5zMAKG-8FK3kJM4rjt`. You can instantly check on the blockchain and see that this account has received more than 5,000 Bitcoins! Knowing that your customer handled $50,000,000 recently, you might be inclined to charge more in the future, or simply rob them now. This privacy issue presents a personal security risk.

In addition to knowing your customers' balances, you can also see every transaction that they have received or sent: the amount, the timestamp, and both participants' addresses. Analysis of transaction activity and history can be used to profile your spending patterns, income, savings, and with whom you interact.

A significant amount of your sensitive personal information can be exposed if your pseudo-anonymous blockchain identity is linked to your real-life identity (for example, during an online purchase or while registering for a cryptocurrency exchange). Often the owner of an account can be revealed with a little bit of research; for instance, you might have already searched for the two Bitcoin addresses listed above to learn that they belong to Satoshi Nakomoto and the Pineapple Fund charity, respectively.

Several companies exist solely to track and deanonymize transparent blockchains. For example, Elliptic offers an interactive explorer that shows the flow of funds between Satoshi, payment processors,

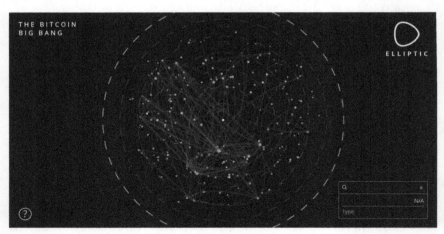

Figure 1.6 - Elliptic's blockchain analysis of Bitcoin flow in the early 2010's, from the interactive Bitcoin Big Bang explorer.

exchanges, forums, marketplaces, gambling services, charities, known individuals, and other services.

Figure 1.6 shows a screenshot detailing significant Bitcoin transactions in the early 2010s, including connections between mining pools, Mt. Gox, and the Silk Road marketplace.

Take a moment to consider the valuable sensitive information that you generate each day: credit card transactions, every phrase that you search, products you view or purchase, social media sites that you interact with, etc... All of this information is routinely recorded and monetized by your banks, payment processors, giant tech/data industries, and governments.

This mass collection of your data results in centralization of your personal and private information in vast troves of sensitive material that are juicy targets for hackers and blackmarket resale. It is quite probable that your personal details (such as name, address, email, phone number, etc) are already in the public domain without your knowledge, perhaps connected with your demographic and/or marketing dossier.

Consider the recent Equifax, Target, Home Depot, Uber, and Panera data breaches. In many cases, both personal and financial information were compromised, putting individuals and their cards at risk.

Accidental data breaches are not the only concern. Big data and tech companies carefully record your activities online, so that they can profile your preferences in order to provide better services. Often, this is used for targeted marketing and ads; however, this data can also be leveraged for more questionable uses such as manipulating your feelings or your voting behavior.

Anything that a company tracks about you may end up stolen, carelessly resold, or used unethically. You should exercise great caution regarding your digital footprint, since information cannot be "unleaked" after your personal details are exposed.

Right now, privacy is conspicuously absent from mainstream economic and commercial systems. Traditional payment processors, banks, and cryptocurrencies leave very clear trails that are used to study, surveil, and profit from you. Once collected, you often have no way to control or track the proliferation of your data, or know of the privacy and personal security risks that arise from its sale to unknown parties.

The only guaranteed way to exercise your right to financial privacy is to avoid revealing personal information in the first place! To stay safe, we need a way to interact securely - where transactions cannot be linked to your identity, your savings, or other transactions. The Monero cryptocurrency is your best tool for taking all of these matters into your own hands!

1.3 Introducing Monero

MONERO (pronounced /mōněrō/, plural *moneroj*) is a leading cryptocurrency with a focus on private and censorship-resistant transactions. The openly verifiable nature of most cryptocurrencies (such as Bitcoin and Ethereum) allows anybody in the world to track your money. Furthermore, links between your financial records and personal identity may jeopardize your safety.

To avoid these dangers, Monero uses powerful cryptographic techniques to create a network that allows parties to interact **without revealing the sender, recipient, or transaction amounts**. Like other cryptocurrencies, Monero has a decentralized ledger that all participants can download and verify for themselves.

However, a series of mathematical tricks are used to conceal all of the sensitive details and stymie any blockchain tracking. Monero's privacy features allow the network to assess the validity of a transaction and determine whether or not the sender has a sufficient account balance, without the actually knowing the transaction amount or account balances! Nobody can view others' account balances, and transactions do not reveal the source of the funds being transferred.

One of Monero's crucial defining features is its philosophy of **enforced privacy by default**. Users are specifically prevented from initializing transactions that are accidentally or intentionally insecure. This provides Monero users with peace of mind since the network will not accept a revealing transaction! **Monero users reap all the benefits of a decentralized trustless financial system, without risking the security and privacy downsides of a transparent blockchain.**

Figure 1.7 (next page) shows how Maria pays George for the car, using Monero. The process is functionally the same as the cryptocurrency transaction shown in **figure 1.5**, however the sensitive information is cryptographically obscured. Information such as account balances and transaction amounts are marked with "***" in the diagram, since no outside observer can ascertain the values. The mechanics behind these unique privacy features are discussed in chapter 3 (conceptual) and chapter 5 (technical).

Figure 1.7 - Maria sends money to George using Monero. The ****'s represent sensitive information, such as addresses and balances, that are masked by Monero's privacy features.

1.3.1 Principles of Monero

Monero is designed with the following principles in mind:

- **Network decentralization:** The Monero network and ledger are distributed globally. There is no single server or database that can be maliciously hacked, controlled, or censored. If one government were to shut down Monero nodes in their country, or attempt to limit who can send/receive Monero, the effort would be in vain! The rest of the world will maintain the network and continue processing transactions.

- **Financial security:** The Monero network is self-secured by incorruptible cryptographic mechanisms, so there is no need to trust a third party with responsibility over your funds and transactions. Every single Monero participant can verify the validity of the ledger themselves, so you do not even need to trust the node operators! (You can learn more about the cryptographic techniques that secure Monero in chapter 5.)

- **Financial privacy:** Most blockchain systems achieve strong security at the expense of privacy. However, Monero prioritizes providing total privacy with no security concessions. Transaction amounts, sender identity, and recipient identity are all obfuscated on the blockchain, so your Monero storage and spending activities are not trackable.

- **Fungibility:** The term *fungibility* refers to assets whose units are considered indistinguishable and interchangeable.. For example, imagine that you let your neighbor borrow 1 kilogram of flour for a cake. When they return flour the next week, of course it will be 1 kilogram of flour from a different source (since they used your original flour for baking). This is not a problem, since flour is fungible. However, vehicles are not fungible; if you let your neighbor borrow your car, you probably want the same one back!

  In the case of Monero, its fungibility is a feature of its sophisticated privacy practices; the obfuscated transaction record obscures the history of all monero.. If you let your friend borrow 1 Monero, they can return any 1 Monero, since they're indistinguishable. This particular quality may seem like a minor nuance; however, fungibility is crucially necessary for most practical uses of any currency (see examples below). This characteristic is absent from most cryptocurrencies, with transparent ledgers and trackable histories.

1.3.2 Real-life "use cases" for Monero

This section talks about some of the difficulties and risks that arise from using insecure cryptocurrencies. **For simplicity, the examples refer to "Bitcoin" as the prototypical transparent-blockchain currency. However, these drawbacks are present in essentially all cryptocurrencies.**

- **Price manipulation:** Sofia is the only mechanic in a small town. One of her customers paid for an oil change with Bitcoin. Sofia later looked up his address on the ledger and saw that the customer's wallet contained enough Bitcoin for a new Lamborghini. Next time he needed a repair, she doubled her prices. If the customer had used Monero, Sofia would have been unable view his balance or use such information to manipulate prices.

- **Financial surveillance:** Oleg's parents send him some Bitcoin to pay for textbooks, then continue to snoop on his Bitcoin address and activity. A few months later, Oleg sends some leftover Bitcoin to the public donation address for an organization that does not align with his parents' political views. He does not realize that they are still monitoring his Bitcoin activity until he receives a furious email from his parents, berating him. If Oleg had used Monero, his family would not have been upset due to prying into his transaction activity.

- **Supply chain privacy:** Kyung-seok owns a small business providing family catering services for local events. A large food company uses blockchain tracing to identify most of his regular clients. The corporation uses this list to contact Kyung-seok's customers, offering similar deals for 5% less. If Kyung-seok's business used Monero instead, its transaction history could not have been exploited by rival businesses seeking to steal his customers.

- **Discrimination:** Ramona finds her dream apartment, conveniently close to her new job in a great neighborhood. Every month, she promptly pays her rent in Bitcoin. However the landlord notices that some of the payments track back to a legal online casino. The landlord personally despises gambling, and unexpectedly chooses to not renew Ramona's lease. If Ramona paid rent with Monero instead, the landlord would not be able to review its history and discriminate based on her legal source of income.

- **Transaction security/privacy:** Sven sells a guitar to a stranger, and gives the buyer a Bitcoin address from his long-term savings wallet. The buyer checks the blockchain, sees the large sum of money that Sven has saved up, and consequently robs him at gunpoint. If Sven had instead given a Monero address for payment, the buyer would not have been able to view Sven's wealth.

- **Tainted coins:** Loki sells some of his artwork online to save up for college. When he pays tuition, he is shocked to receive a "payment INVALID" error from the school. Unbeknownst to Loki, one of his paintings was purchased using some Bitcoin that was stolen during an exchange hack the previous year. Since the school rejects any payment from a blacklist of "tainted" Bitcoins, they refuse to mark the bill "paid." Loki is in an extremely difficult position: the Bitcoin that he saved has already been transferred out of his account, yet the tuition bill is still unpaid. This entire situation would have been avoided if Loki sold his paintings for Monero instead, since its fungibility precludes tracking or blacklists.

These examples have shown how Monero's privacy features keep users safe from snooping family, tainted coins, and unethical business practices. All cryptocurrencies are a relatively new technology, and there is no such thing as "perfect privacy." If keeping a particular payment secret is a matter of life and death, it may be risky to use *any* cryptocurrency for that transaction.

1.3.3 Monero: open-source decentralized community and software

Monero is an open-source project actively developed by cryptography and distributed systems experts from all over the world. Many of these developers freely donate their time to The Monero Project. Others are funded by the Monero community so that they can focus entirely on the project.

The decentralized nature of Monero's development team brings several benefits over a consolidated corporation or organization. The Monero Project is a living entity greater than any individual or group. Since both the network and development team are spread across the globe, it cannot be shut down by any single country.

The term *open-source* means that the source code (software blueprints) are made publicly available for anybody to inspect. The alternative is *closed-source* software, where developers only deliver the final compiled product (*binaries* such as .exe files) that cannot be opened and studied. If you use closed-source software, you are trusting the developer and distributor. The problem is that even a developer with the best intentions may make a mistake that hackers later discover and exploit. Only use open-source cryptocurrency software that has been audited by independent parties to verify absence of malicious code, accidental mistakes, and implementation weaknesses.

The cryptocurrency community has embraced open-source software from the very start: Bitcoin was released as a public white paper and open-source community-built code, which stood in stark contrast to the opaque and proprietary decision structure endemic to fiat (government-backed) currencies. Of course, the open-source philosophy has been around much longer than cryptocurrencies! Over 25 years, more than 5,000 coders have contributed to the open-source Linux kernel, which is widely considered to be one of the most secure operating systems.

The trust and security benefits of open-source software are of key importance for any cryptocurrency, so The Monero Project is entirely open-source. The developers use GitHub for version control, which allows anybody to easily review every single line of code proposed to be added, removed, or modified. Over 240 developers have contributed to, reviewed, and tested the Monero code, which drastically lowers the likelihood that any errors have been overlooked. Developers can find more information about interacting with Monero's codebase in chapters 6 and 7.

Development team transparency is very important for community trust, especially for cryptocurrencies. Monero development discussion occurs in open IRC channels, and the Monero Project website hosts public archives of meeting logs.

1.3.4 History of Monero

In 2013 Nicolas van Saberhagen published the "CryptoNote" protocol, which became the foundation for many coins, starting with Bytecoin. Like Bitcoin's Satoshi Nakamoto, the creator of Bytecoin remained anonymous and promoted their coin through a Bitcointalk thread.

Some aspects of Bytecoin appeared dubious under close scrutiny. Bitcointalk member *"thankful_for_today"* investigated the emissions curve and noted that approximately 82% of the coins had already been emitted, so the circulating coin supply was potentially dangerously centralized.

Ultimately, this greedy premine undermined Bytecoin's credibility and practicality. Thankfully, thankful_for_today recognized the value in CryptoNote's features, and incorporated them into a new project centered around a strong, community-driven development team. The Monero cryptocurrency, spearheaded by thankful_for_today, launched in April 2014. The coin was originally named "BitMonero," however the community quickly elected to shorten it to "Monero," which is the word for "coin" in the Esperanto language.

1.3.5 Ethical discussion

Monero was carefully engineered to provide characteristics like fungibility and transaction privacy that are necessary for any currency (crypto- or otherwise) to be feasible for general use. As discussed in the section "Real-life 'use cases' for Monero," there are significant practical issues that arise with financial systems that do not protect users' privacy.

The very features necessary to keep Monero safe for day-to-day users and businesses are unfortunately also appealing to those wishing to conceal illicit activity. Monero is not specifically designed to facilitate illegal activity, which has plagued every currency since the idea of money was conceived thousands of years ago. The scale of illegal transactions conducted using cryptocurrencies is dwarfed by the staggeringly-vast amount of criminal activity that occurs every day denominated in fiat currencies like Euros, Rupees, Yen, or Dollars.

Monero mining is designed to be compatible with computers, phones, tablets, and most web browsers; this allows anybody to easily enter the mining ecosystem with no barriers from equipment costs. Unfortunately, hackers have taken advantage of this accessibility to create exploitative websites and software that secretly mine Monero for the attacker. Nonconsensual mining is tantamount to theft of resources, and the Monero community recently self-organized a team of volunteers to freely assist victims. The Malware Response Workgroup provides education, tools, and live support to combat software that employs Monero for malicious mining and ransomware.

The creators of *Mastering Monero* are excited about the currency's use for widespread personal, retail, and commercial applications. We hope that our readers use Monero ethically and often! You can discover online stores that accept Monero through Project Coral Reef. There are several websites that make it easy to use your equipment to philanthropically mine Monero to support various non-profits, such as UNICEF Australia, BailBloc, and Change.org.

Getting started: receiving, storing and sending Monero

T he last chapter focused on WHY to use Monero; in this chapter you will learn HOW to use Monero. You can master Monero without needing to learn any of the complex cryptographic or technical network details, so that extra information is saved for later in the book. Chapter 2 will cover all the practical skills you'll need to get started receiving, storing, and spending your moneroj.

The first part of this chapter covers key concepts and terminology for Monero use, as general information that will apply to any wallet or software. Toward the end of the chapter, you'll find handy guides for carrying out these steps using the free official open-source Monero command line interface (CLI) or graphical user interface (GUI) software.

2.1 What is a wallet?

Before you obtain some moneroj, you must plan ahead for where you will receive and store your funds. You will need a *wallet* to help you store and spend your moneroj. Your current paper money (e.g. euros or dollars) can be stored in many different styles of physical wallets. Likewise, there are several different types of Monero wallets, and you can always move some of your money from an old wallet to a new one.

Wallets take care of the complicated cryptographic processes for you, so you don't need to know any fancy mathematics to use Monero. You will only need to manage a seed and your address(es), and learn how to navigate the functionality of your chosen wallet. Other details like *public keys* and *private keys* are managed behind-the-scenes by your wallet, so they are not discussed until chapter 5.

Your Monero seed is a secret number that your wallet uses to locate and spend your moneroj, though it is converted into a series of 12-25+ words for convenience. This secret is like a treasure map to your money on the blockchain, and anybody who learns your seed can use their wallet to access and spend your moneroj. For this reason, you must be extremely careful when you generate and store your seed. Do not set up a wallet in a coffee shop, where other patrons or cameras may see your secret. It is dangerous to store your seed electronically (e.g. in a text file or email) since malicious software or services may be able to obtain it, and run off with your moneroj.

Your seed is used to generate your address(es) for receiving moneroj. Just like your postal address, you share your Monero address with people who want to send you something. Most wallets will show your address in two different formats - a written string of numbers/letters, and a visual QR code. You can safely share either of these when you wish to give someone one of your addresses so that they can send you monero.

If your Monero wallet is physically damaged, you can simply import your seed into a new wallet, and pick up right where you left off! As long as you have a copy of your seed, you can always access your funds. However, **if you lose your seed, there is no way to ever recover access to your moneroj**. You may be familiar with passwords, which can usually be reset by contacting an administrator. **Seeds are not like passwords** - nobody else knows your secret, and the network is unable to shift your moneroj to a new account if you lose your seed.

Most software will prompt you to write down the seed when you initialize a new wallet. However some apps skip this reminder, and you must take the initiative to find the backup feature and write down your seed. Be sure to do this immediately, or else a damaged device will cause you to permanently lose your funds.

Figure 2.1 - Wallets carry out all of the key functions for using Monero.

2.2 Selecting the best wallet(s) for your needs

In this section, you'll learn about different types of wallets available for storing your moneroj.

You probably store most of your local currency (e.g. euros or dollars) in a bank or safe, and carry around a small amount in your day-to-day physical wallet. Likewise, many people use two complementary wallet types for their cryptocurrency: a convenient *hot wallet* that holds small amounts for day-to-day use, complemented by a more secure *cold wallet* for long-term savings or large amounts.

There are various storage solutions, and they vary in terms of convenience, privacy, and security. Your individual needs will determine which type(s) of wallets are best for you. The varying wallet types described below differ primarily in where the seed is stored.

2.2.1 Software and mobile wallets

Software wallets (on a desktop computer or mobile device) are convenient for storing and using Monero. Many Monero users have a handy hot wallet on their phones, to pay for day-to-day purchases. A good rule of thumb is to only walk around carrying as much cryptocurrency as you would feel comfortable holding in regular cash. Software wallets store the secret seed on your device, so your moneroj could be stolen if you catch a virus or keylogger.

Figure 2.2.a - Monerujo (Android Wallet)

Figure 2.2.b - Cake wallet (iOS Wallet)

2.2.2 Hardware wallets

Hardware wallets are physical devices that can carry out sensitive wallet functions, completely isolated from the connected phone or computer. Hardware wallets have their own built-in screens, to show you the seed and transaction details without ever sending them to an external device!

While hardware wallets are less convenient than software wallets, they are extremely secure! Because of how they store and protect your seed, you can safely use a hardware wallet to send transactions from a device that you suspect or know is compromised with malicious software. The Monero community is currently developing "Kastelo" - the first open-source cryptocurrency hardware wallet.

Figure 2.3 -Kastelo is an open-source hardware wallet for Monero

2.2.3 Paper wallets

Paper wallets provide an inexpensive way to stash moneroj that you do not plan to move frequently. You simply print out a physical copy of your public and secret information for safe storage. Since the secrets from your Monero seed are saved only on paper, not digitally, you do not have to worry about viruses or data leaks. However, paper wallets are not convenient for frequent use, since you must transfer the secrets to a digital device every time you wish to send moneroj.

Figure 2.4 - A paper wallet is a printed copy of your Monero keys. Make sure nobody sees the secret information!

2.2.4 Web wallets

Web wallets are Monero accounts that you access through a website hosted by some third party. These online wallets are extremely convenient, however this comes at the expense of your security and privacy. There are essentially two types of web wallets - the crucial difference is whether or not you know the seed.

The first type of web wallet stores the money in their own accounts and gives you a username and password to log in (note: this includes your "wallets" on exchanges). Since you do not have the seed yourself, you do not personally control your funds; you must trust the service to hold your money for you. You should be extremely wary of storing moneroj in these types of web wallets, which are essentially providing banking services. They might lose your funds at any time, whether through accident or theft. If the website is shut down, your username and password are useless - since you don't have the seed yourself, your funds are gone.

The second type of web wallet instead leaves the seed and funds in only your control. Well-designed web wallets, such as MyMonero, use secure methods to access your funds without ever sending your secret seed to the third-party server. You must enter your seed every time you log in, because it is not known to the provider or stored on your device. This type of web wallet is (relatively) safer, since the third party is not holding your funds. They are only providing a software interface for your browser. If the website for this type of wallet becomes inaccessible, you can enter your seed into a different wallet and fully recover your funds.

While web wallets are convenient, neither type is recommended for long-term storage or large amounts. Both types have security downsides (trusting your funds to a third party, or frequently typing your seed into a web browser) and there are potential privacy concessions in both cases.

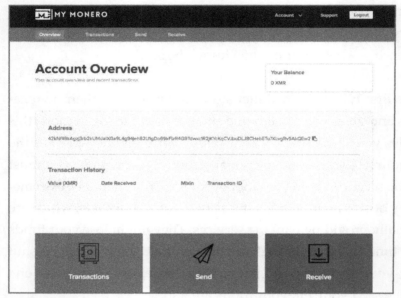

Figure 2.5 - MyMonero Interface.

2.2.5 Cold wallets

The phrase cold wallet is an umbrella term that is used to refer to paper wallets and other offline storage methods. For example, an electronic cold wallet can be a phone or computer that is only used for interacting with cryptocurrencies, and is disconnected from the internet except when in use. The device can use any operating system; the important part is deliberate implementation of strong security practices (including a firewall, antivirus software, and extreme caution regarding accessing only trusted websites/software). The seed is still on the computer, however you keep the device sequestered from the rest of the world as much as possible.

Figure 2.6 - A cold wallet refers to a secured device, intended only for storing and transacting with cryptocurrencies. A computer running the Monero command line interface is shown above, as an example.

2.2.6 Monero wallet links

Regardless of which type(s) of wallet you choose, be careful to only download vetted software through proper channels. Phishing schemes and scam wallets are numerous, so be sure to double-check that you are installing legitimate software! If you enter your seed into a malicious wallet, your moneroj will be gone before you even realize your mistake.

This section contains links to several **open-source** wallets that are developed and trusted by the Monero community.

LIGHTWEIGHT WALLETS:
* <u>Monerujo</u> - Android
* <u>Cake Wallet</u> - iOS
* <u>Mymonero.com</u> - Web Wallet, Desktop, Android and iOS

OFFICIAL SOFTWARE:
* Graphic User Interface (GUI) - <u>Windows</u>, <u>Mac</u> and <u>Linux</u>
* Command Line Interface (CLI) - <u>Windows</u>, <u>Mac</u> and <u>Linux</u>

2.2.7 Connecting to a remote node (optional)

You can reduce sync time and disk usage by connecting to a *remote node* instead of storing the entire blockchain on your device. Most mobile wallets, such as the lightweight apps listed above, are automatically configured to connect to a default remote node. If you need to manually direct your software to a remote node, you can use the community resources at `node.moneroworld.com` (port `18089`).

Nodes are computers that have downloaded the entire blockchain, and assist other users by syncing their wallets and relaying their transactions. Running your own (local) node is best for privacy, and you can choose to share your node publically if you wish to help secure the network. Remote nodes are convenient, and allow you to begin using Monero quickly, without downloading the entire blockchain.

Running a node is not the same as *mining* Monero. Mining is a different resource-intensive process, not discussed until Chapter 4. Once the blockchain is synced, running a local node is not heavy on CPU or network resources.

2.3 Using Monero

This section explains what you need to know for sending and receiving Monero. All of the examples in this book use the following seed:

```
MASTERING MONERO DEMO SEED: lamb hexagon aces
acquire  twang  bluntly  argue  when  unafraid
awning  academy  nail  threaten  sailor  palace
selfish cadets click sickness juggled border
thumbs remedy ridges border
```

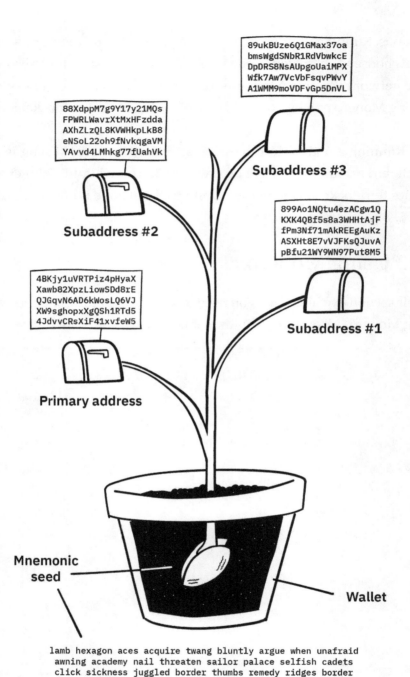

89ukBUze6Q1GMax37oa
bmsWgdSNbR1RdVbwkcE
DpDRS8NsAUpgoUaiMPX
Wfk7Aw7VcVbFsqvPWvY
A1WMM9moVDFvGp5DnVL

Subaddress #3

88XdppM7g9Y17y21MQs
FPWRLWavrXtMxHFzdda
AXhZLzQL8KVWHkpLkB8
eNSoL22oh9fNvkqgaVM
YAvvd4LMhkg77fUahVk

Subaddress #2

899Ao1NQtu4ezACgw1Q
KXK4QBf5s8a3WHHtAjF
fPm3Nf71mAkREEgAuKz
ASXHt8E7vVJFKsQJuvA
pBfu21WY9WN97Put8M5

Subaddress #1

4BKjy1uVRTPiz4pHyaX
Xawb82XpzLiowSDd8rE
QJGqvN6AD6kWosLQ6VJ
XW9sghopxXgQSh1RTd5
4JdvvCRsXiF41xvfeW5

Primary address

**Mnemonic
seed**

Wallet

lamb hexagon aces acquire twang bluntly argue when unafraid
awning academy nail threaten sailor palace selfish cadets
click sickness juggled border thumbs remedy ridges border

Figure 2.7 - Wallets use the secret seed to generate addresses for receiving
Monero.

44

You can import this seed yourself to practice generating addresses, checking transaction history, and verifying payments. You can use this seed to follow along with examples in the book, but do not send your monero to it! Anybody else reading *Mastering Monero* will be able to spend it!

2.3.1 Receiving Monero

To receive Monero, all you have to do is share your wallet address with the person sending you moneroj. Most wallets will show your address in two formats: an alphanumeric string that is easy to copy & paste, and a QR code that is handy for scanning with a camera. Here are examples of both formats, from the DEMO seed above:

 Your address for receiving Monero can be represented as a text string, or QR code. You can share whichever is more convenient. In the example, we have 4BKjy1uVRTPiz4pHyaXXawb82Xp-zLiowSDd8rEQJGqvN6AD6kWosLQ6VJXW9sghopxXgQSh1RT-d54JdvvCRsXiF41xvfeW5

This address that you share is never stored on the blockchain (thanks to a Monero feature known as *stealth addresses*, which are discussed conceptually in chapter 3 and described technically in chapter 5). Monero also allows you to generate multiple *subaddresses* from your single secret seed, so you can share many different addresses that all deposit to the same wallet.

Each Monero account has a single primary address (starting with a '4'). For convenience, you can generate an unlimited number of subaddresses (starting with an '8'). Funds received by any of the addresses are routed to your wallet's main balance. You can learn more about the how your wallet handles multiple addresses in Chapter 5.

Wallets may wait 10 - 20 minutes for *confirmation* before marking funds as received and safe to spend (you can learn why in Chapter 4). This is a common security practice, and wallets usually show the unconfirmed transaction during the waiting period. If your wallet is waiting for a 0.06 XMR payment to confirm, you may see something like the image below.

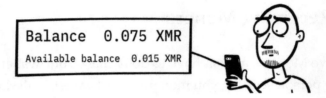

There is no need for concern when this occurs! Within less than a half hour, the funds will confirm and transfer to your available balance.

Monero supports the ability to share a *view-only* version of your wallet, which can see all incoming transactions but cannot send or view outgoing funds. This feature has many important uses: enabling full transparency for charity donations, providing access to financial records for authorized auditors, and creation of limited-access devices to monitor incoming payments. Initializing a view-only wallet involves sharing a *secret view key*, which is different from the secret seed; this intermediate topic is covered in chapter 5.

2.3.2 Sending Monero

To send Monero, you simply enter or scan the recipient's address, and type the amount that you wish to transfer. Press "send" and your transaction will be initiated!

If you are sending moneroj to a business, they may also ask you to include a *payment ID* to connect your payment to your order. If you are sending moneroj to yourself or a friend, you can leave the payment ID field blank. Some services use "integrated addresses", which include the payment ID and address in a single text string for convenience and increased privacy.

In 2018, Monero added the ability for each wallet to generate a vast number of *subaddresses* for receiving payments. Consequently, payment IDs and integrated addresses are being used less frequently. Instead of giving each customer the same address but different payment IDs, modern merchants simply give each customer a unique subaddress (this system is more straightforward and has less room for "user error").

Anybody using the free OpenAlias system can provide a human-readable Monero address (e.g. "donate.getmonero.org") instead of the raw address string (44AFFq5k....). Sending to an OpenAlias address is no different than sending to the raw address. However, setting up a new OpenAlias address is a more technical task, covered in chapter 7.

Your wallet will add a small fee, to compensate the network for forwarding and processing your transaction. Your wallet will recommend an appropriate fee based on the current Monero network load, your transaction's urgency, and a few other behind-the-scenes considerations. You can learn more about how fees work and why they are necessary to maintain the network in Chapter 4.

2.3.3 How to check proof of payment

Given Monero's anonymity, you might wonder how somebody

can prove that a payment was sent. Besides optional payment IDs, Monero has a second feature to selectively reveal proof that funds were sent. This is accomplished by sharing a *transaction key* that only the true sender can generate.

Example

Suppose your friends Khan and Maria each owe you 0.06552376 XMR for a meal that you split. You only receive 1 payment, with the information below:

Amount: 0.06552376 XMR
Transaction ID:
4b540773ddf9e819f0df47708f3d3c9f7f62933150b90ed-
c89103d36d42ca4b7

Received to (your) sub-address:
899Ao1NQtu4ezACgw1QKXK4QBf5s8a3WHHtAjFfPm3Nf-
71mAkREEgAuKzASXHt8E7vVJFKsQJuvApBfu21WY9WN97Put8M5

This is a real transaction received by the DEMO wallet on 20-Apr 2018. You can see some information through a blockchain explorer, however the Monero sender is always unknown. Both Khan and Maria claim that they sent the payment, so you ask each to provide the transaction key.

Khan:
OutProofV1N4Y5pUJEnRACJyB5C3zK1zTqAihdn-
N8MfVZhEWfD13Z2N7Npt1uxa1EY7N7jnvuJF76tXU-
wKrakvZSxTj4Zux5SpavFb4X1jRcLAJ2b5hqviQPiS-
58j2qH53QL44CJEgHtY5

Maria:

OutProofV1To53Qu2gegZbUevosKCTwrEdqiECgFyUygutX-
MEdhrHg1EtXMrFNaszWYFjdU4aXFZ2iPF8G8jzoDJzCoW5d-
sWvb4mVN65abAya3U47cGXs7WABrTzG5aPfV4YBANhwPgwD2

When you check both of their transaction keys, Maria's confirms payment to your address and Khan's key returns "bad signature." You can practice this yourself using the above address and transaction keys!

2.4 Operational security

Figure 2.8 - Phishing attacks often use slightly-different URLs to trick users into entering their seeds or passwords into an attacker's copy of the real site (for example, www.mymonera.com instead of www.mymonero.com). Always carefully inspect the URL, especially when following links.

Monero allows you to **be your own bank**, since nobody can control your funds besides you! This grassroots financial empowerment is one of the greatest benefits of cryptocurrencies. However, with great power comes great responsibility! Keeping operational security (OpSec) in mind is important for keeping yourself and your funds safe.

2.4.1 Never say how much Monero you own

Sayings like "loose lips sink ships" exist for a reason. When you publicly disclose about how much Monero you have, you may inadvertently make yourself a target for scams or theft. This is especially true in cases of online forums and social media.

Scammers and thieves prowl the internet looking for individuals who have revealed exploitable information about themselves and their wealth.

Most people know better than to post about the balance of their bank account or retirement portfolio on social media. It is a security risk, rude, and can make interpersonal relationships awkward when wealth imbalances are involved. However, lots of people naively declare how much Bitcoin or Monero they have bought.

Remember that cryptocurrency prices are volatile, and are known to increase dramatically. A post stating "I just spent $50 on Bitcoin in case it lasts" from 2012 may have seemed modest at the time, however that $50 (~10 BTC in 2012) was worth nearly a million dollars by the end of 2017, less than 5 years later! Messages on the internet can be hard to erase, so the best way to avoid this situation is never posting in the first place.

Given the general interest in cryptocurrency investing, there is lots of conversation about holdings and portfolio composition. You should always talk in percentages rather than absolute amounts. Figure (below) shows how to calculate your portfolio balances, so you can discuss your saving strategies without revealing sensitive information.

PORTFOLIO

Cryptocurrency	Quantity		Exchange Rate		Value		Percentage
ABC	0.1	X	1150€	=	115€	=	23%
XMR	1.1	X	200€	=	220€	=	44%
WYZ	3300	X	0.05€	=	165€	=	33%
					500€		100%

HOW TO TALK ABOUT IT

2.4.2 Keeping your seed safe

Your funds are only as safe as your seed, and there are two major concerns to keep in mind: loss due to accident, and loss due to theft.

To avoid the loss due to accident, always make sure your seed is backed up somewhere secure. Always ask yourself: "If my phone dies or this website breaks, do I have a way to access my funds?" You should consider keeping a second written copy of the seed in a second safe location. You don't want to lose both your device and your backup seed if your house floods or burns.

To avoid loss due to theft, never share your seed or keys with anybody else. Anyone with access to your seed can steal 100% of your funds, and Monero's privacy features will make it impossible for you to determine where they went.

2.4.3 Transaction precautions

When sending any large transaction to a new person or exchange, you should always initially test the address/service by sending a smaller amount first. When sending any large transaction to a new person or address, you should always send a tiny pilot transaction first and wait for the recipient to confirm that it arrived. This is an important habit to catch mistakes in advance, since there is no "undo" button for cryptocurrencies.

With every cryptocurrency transaction, always double-check the wallet addresses to make sure that it is correct. Even if you copy & paste the address, visually confirm that it was pasted correctly and in its entirety. Hackers have created malware that manipulates cryptocurrency addresses in the clipboard (replacing the true recipient's address with the attackers's). If you visually double-check the address, you can catch this malware before you make a "donation" to a hacker.

2.4.4 Exchange safety

Exchanges create their own wallets for you, and generally do not share the seed with you. This is risky, since you have no way to recover your money if the exchange is attacked, shut down, or otherwise disappears. There is a famous saying "Not your keys? Not your Bitcoin!" referring to wallets and services that retain control over your keys, and thus your funds.

As mentioned in 2.4.2, you should always be asking yourself "if this website disappears, do I have a way to access my funds?" A good rule of thumb is to only keep your moneroj on an exchange if you plan to trade it soon. Otherwise, move it to a wallet that you control.

2.5 Getting started for businesses

2.5.1 Monero is ideal for merchants

In this chapter, we covered all of the key skills for general Monero use. This section introduces a few extra tools for helping merchants integrate Monero into their systems and services. You can skip ahead to the next chapter if you are not involved with incoming business payments.

Merchants accepting payment in Monero benefit from fast, private, and irreversible transactions. There are several tools designed to ensure that accepting Monero is a "user-friendly" experience for both online and brick-and-mortar businesses.

Of course, anybody can use the general skills from the last chapter to set up a wallet and begin receiving Monero immediately. However the tools mentioned in this chapter are designed to facilitate use by businesses that wish to automate payment integration and processes like issuing invoices and receipts.

2.5.2 Friendly tools for accepting Monero

The Monero Integrations payment gateway allows any online shop to add a Monero payment option by simply installing any one of the plugins designed for several popular content management systems. The Monero Integrations solution was created (by the author of this book) to be consistent with the Monero ethos: the entire project is free, open source, decentralized, and private. Transactions are routed directly to your wallet, so there are none of the privacy or security concessions that arise when trusting a third party to process payments.

Kasisto was the first point of sale system that accepted Monero, and is an open-source project requiring no third parties. The application is intended for in-store use on a phone or tablet, and can accept payments nearly instantly by detecting transactions before they have even been mined. You can try a demo at the Kasisto GitHub.

Another payment option is GloBee, which allows merchants to accept both cryptocurrency and credit card payments. GloBee is a third-party company, which allows them to provide additional functionality - for example, accepting many types of coins with instant settlement into Monero, other cryptocurrencies, and even fiat accounts (e.g. euros or dollars). This gives your business the option to accept cryptocurrencies and be paid immediately in your local fiat currency, eliminating exposure to price volatility risk.

If you want to dive into coding and build your own payment options from scratch, you can learn all about creating the backend in Chapter 7.

## Chapter 3

How Monero works

T he first two chapters covered everything you need to know about WHY to use Monero (Chapter 1) and HOW to use Monero (Chapter 2). By now, you have learned everything necessary to begin using Monero yourself!

The rest of this book contains extra details, for those wishing to dive deeper into how Monero works "behind the scenes." **Chapters 3 and 4** describe underlying technologies such as **Monero's privacy features, the blockchain, and the mining process** - focusing on understanding the concepts, **without digressing into the advanced mathematics**. Later chapters contain those nitty-gritty details for developers and cryptography geeks.

3.1 Transaction and the ledger

To set the stage for understanding Monero's privacy technologies, we will consider how moneroj are sent and received on the ledger. For this chapter, we will focus on *blockchain functionality* - its role as an inherently tamper-proof shared database that keeps a list of Monero transactions. The details about *blockchain security* (mining, hashes, etc) are another topic, reserved for Chapter 4.

When you set up a wallet for the first time, it generates a new *seed* that you will keep secret and use to access your moneroj on the blockchain. This initialization process is carried out on your device, and can be executed entirely offline; nothing is broadcast to, or recorded by, the network during wallet generation.

Behind the scenes, your wallet calculates two sets of keys from your seed. Your *private keys* are a closely-guarded secret, since you use them to prove your identity and access your moneroj. Your *public keys* are, as the name implies, made known to other Monero users. Public and private keys are generated together as sets, with particular mathematical properties that create a special link between the keys.

To receive moneroj, you give your address (created from your public keys) to the sender. When somebody (a customer, an exchange, or a friend) sends you Monero, they will broadcast a transaction that transfers some of their moneroj into a new entry on the ledger that you (and only you) can unlock with your private keys.

In technical lingo, the *output* of their transaction is stored on the blockchain for you to access and spend with your private keys, at your leisure. This terminology can be a bit confusing, since the cryptocurrency use of the word "output" has a different meaning than its typical definition.

Each time you receive moneroj, you gain another output; each time you spend moneroj, you use up one of your outputs and generate a new one for somebody else. In fact, all of the moneroj that you "own" are simply outputs on the blockchain that your private keys unlock. Until somebody sends you moneroj, there will not be any outputs on the blockchain that are associated with, or accessible by, your private keys.

When your wallet is *scanning* or *syncing* this usually means that it is using your private keys to check all of the transactions and outputs on the blockchain to identify relevant entries. Your wallet *balance* is the total sum of these outputs that your private keys can unlock and spend.

When you send moneroj from your wallet, you use up some of your outputs as *inputs* to a transaction that you broadcast to the network. Conceptually, the blockchain is simply a record of these transactions, each consuming the sender's outputs as inputs, to generate a new output for the recipient.

The process described above is slightly simplified, to convey the crucial parts (private/public keys, transactions, inputs/outputs). The following sections provide non-technical explanations of the key concepts underlying Monero's suite of privacy features.

3.2 Privacy technology overview

The general principles and terminology introduced above are shared by most cryptocurrencies. Monero provides enhanced functionality and privacy through several unique cryptographic technologies that shield the users and their activity from public visibility.
Figure 3.1 shows how these complementary features work together to protect sensitive transaction details:

- **RingCT** conceals the transaction amount.

- **Ring signatures** protect the sender by obfuscating which output was spent.

- **Stealth address** ensure that the recipient's address is not recorded on the blockchain.

- **Kovri** breaks the link between your transactions and physical location by obfuscating the broadcast origin and concealing network signs of Monero activity.

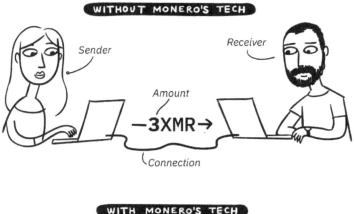

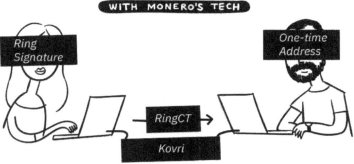

Figure 3.1 - Monero's several privacy technologies work together to conceal all sensitive information generated with a transaction.

3.2.1 Ring Confidential Transactions

RingCT is a cryptographic technology that conceals the amount of moneroj being sent in any transaction. With most cryptocurrencies, transaction amounts are sent in cleartext, visible to any observer. RingCT keeps this sensitive information private by allowing the sender to prove that they have enough moneroj for a transaction, **without revealing the value of that amount!** This is possible thanks to cryptographic *commitments* and *range proofs*.

When you send moneroj, you "commit" the amount in a private way, revealing just enough information for the network to confirm the legitimacy of the transaction, while not publicly disclosing the amount itself. A valid commitment guarantees that the transaction is not fraudulently creating or overspending moneroj.

Range proofs are another important mechanism in RingCT, as a method to ensure that the committed amount is greater than zero, and less than a certain number. This is necessary to prevent senders from committing negative or impossibly-high amounts of moneroj. Together, commitments and range proofs secure the supply of moneroj against fraudulent manipulation and counterfeiting attempts.

Prior to RingCT, Monero transactions were partitioned into specific denominations (for example, 12.5 XMR would be sent as 10 XMR + 2 XMR + 0.5 XMR) and the transaction amounts were visible to outside observers. RingCT was activated in January 2017, and rapid widespread adoption immediately followed. Within 1 month of its activation, approximately 98% of new transactions were already voluntarily using the RingCT protocol!

In keeping with Monero's policy of enforced privacy-by-default, **RingCT became mandatory for all Monero transactions after September 2017**. To spend any old pre-RingCT outputs, they must first be converted to RingCT outputs with masked amounts.

3.2.2 Stealth (one-time) addresses

All Monero transactions utilize *stealth addresses* to protect the privacy of the recipient. To avoid recording the recipient's wallet address onto the blockchain, each Monero transaction is instead sent to a unique disposable **one-time** address. The recipient can access funds sent to a stealth address, without exposing any links to their wallet's public addresses or other transactions.

Figure 3.2 - A Monero sender's wallet generates a disposable one-time stealth address from the recipient's public address. Only the stealth address will be included in the transaction and blockchain.

To conceptualize the use of random one-time codes to protect the recipient's identity, imagine that you wish to give a few books about coping with a sensitive illness to your friend André. Unfortunately you're about to leave town for a trip and André won't be around until next week. Perhaps you could ask your friendly neighbor to temporarily hold onto the books and pass them forward to the recipient.

Your neighbor will need to verify that anybody attempting to claim the books is actually the intended recipient. Since your friend is a private person with a sensitive condition, it would be inappropriate to tell your neighbor to check their ID for the name "André". How could you arrange the exchange while preserving André's privacy? You could simply make up a one-time random code and tell your neighbor to give the books to whoever presents that code (e.g. give these books to the person who knows the phrase "`PolarComboTango357`"). Your neighbor will be able to keep track of the books and give them to André, without learning anything about their recipient.

Similar to the way you might use that random non-informative code to keep your neighbor from learning about your books' recipient, Monero uses a system of one-time codes to prevent the the network from learning about Monero recipients! Instead of explicitly recording the recipient's address on the blockchain (analogously, "give the books to André"), funds are always sent to a one-time "stealth address" (analogously, "give these books to the person who knows the phrase `PolarComboTango357`"). The cryptographic techniques that secure stealth addresses solely for the recipient are discussed in chapter 5, however the salient points are detailed below.

How are these one-time addresses generated? Your Monero wallet's public addresses are 95-character strings, which incorporate two public keys (the *public view* and *public spend* keys) mathematically derived from your seed. When somebody sends you funds, they will use the public keys in your address along with some random data to generate a unique one-time public key. These one-time public keys that are recorded in transactions on the blockchain are named *stealth addresses* because it is impossible for the network or an outside observer to connect these random codes back to the originating wallets.

Figure 3.3 - On a transparent blockchain, such as Bitcoin, all transactions to the same public address can be easily linked and viewed. Monero's stealth addresses are unlinkable and are never duplicated, so the recipient's financial activity is not visible to other users and senders.

Note that subaddresses are not the same as stealth addresses. Subaddresses are reusable public wallet addresses that are not recorded in the blockchain. Multiple transactions sent to a single subaddress will all point to different and unlinkable stealth addresses.

Improved privacy by not recording wallet addresses on the blockchain is a clear benefit of implementing stealth addresses. An even bigger implication is that use of these unique one-time keys prevents multiple payments to the same address from being linked together!

Suppose you create some public art and post an address for cryptocurrency donations. If you use a coin with a transparent blockchain (e.g. Bitcoin), then every incoming transaction to that address is permanently recorded in searchable linkable form. Anybody can use a blockchain explorer to see how many Bitcoin donations you received, their amount, and whether or not you've moved the funds. Every incoming Bitcoin transaction is indexed on the ledger by the address that you shared publicly.

If you post a Monero address instead, your donations are not exposed to public scrutiny. Each donor will generate a unique one-time stealth address, and record that on the ledger. The public donation address that you posted next to your project will never be directly referenced in a transaction, and the stealth addresses do not provide any information about the recipient. Since each donor mixes in their own random information to create the stealth address for their transaction, one donor cannot recognize a stealth address generated by another.

All Monero transactions must use stealth addresses, to ensure privacy for the entire network. Your wallet automatically creates the stealth address from the public address when it generates the transaction.

3.2.3 Ring signatures

Ring signatures are a Monero feature designed to protect a transaction's sender by obfuscating the source of the moneroj being spent. Before jumping into ring signatures, we'll introduce the concept of digital signatures in general.

Digital signatures are a general cryptographic method for confirming the authenticity and source of data or a message. The signatures can be checked against the public key to confirm the identity of the signer, and verify that the signed message is complete and unmodified. If the signed data is changed by even a single character (whether due to intentional tampering or accidental miscommunication) the signature will be rendered invalid.

Varying implementations of digital signatures are a key component of all cryptocurrencies. To spend one of your outputs, you compose a message to the network describing the transaction, *sign* it with your corresponding private key, then broadcast the result to the network. Before executing the transaction, the network checks the validity of the signature to verify that the message has not been altered, and/or forged, by a third party that does not possess the correct private key.

With transparent cryptocurrencies (e.g. Bitcoin) each message describing a transaction explicitly declares which outputs are being spent. This is useful for easy bookkeeping, since the network simply maintains a record of unspent transaction outputs (UTXOs) that are considered as valid inputs for new transactions. If somebody attempts to spend the same Bitcoin output twice, the fraudulent second transaction is promptly rejected, since the network knows that the owner already spent that output (when they signed and broadcast the first transaction). Unfortunately, this straightforward proof of ownership is highly detrimental to privacy by definitively indicating the source of funds, and indicating when a given output is spent.

Monero uses a different scheme, known as *ring signatures*. This group-signing method allows one member to digitally sign the message on behalf of the group, while mixing in the public keys of the other members, so that it is unclear who actively signed the message. It is possible to cryptographically verify that one of the *ring members* signed the message, but impossible to determine which of the members actually crafted the signature.

Ring signatures are used in Monero to blend the keys from multiple outputs on the blockchain, in order to obfuscate which output is actually being spent. Suppose Maria wants to spend one of her Monero outputs. Her wallet will semi-randomly select several other past outputs on the blockchain (not belonging to Maria) and mix their public keys into the ring signature as *decoys*. The network is able to verify that one of the outputs is being spent, however the decoys and true spender are cryptographically indistinguishable.

Ring signatures protect the sender in all transactions, since the recipient and Monero network are unable to ascertain which ring member is the true source of the funds. A significant consequence of ring signatures is that an outside observer is unable to definitively prove that an output has been spent! The fact that an output appears in a ring signature is entirely inconclusive, since it is impossible to distinguish whether it was truly being spent, or simply passively employed as a decoy ring member.

Since it is impossible to tell whether a particular output has been spent, you might be wondering what prevents an unscrupulous user from trying to spend the same output twice? With one-output-one-spend transparent blockchains (e.g. Bitcoin) this is a trivial task: any output that has been cryptographically signed and transferred once is marked as spent and cannot be used again. However, Monero outputs can appear in ring signatures before and after they have been spent, so output reuse must be prevented by other means.

This is accomplished by utilizing *key images* that are generated and recorded with each transaction, uniquely derived from the actual output being spent. The network cannot ascertain which ring member is connected to the key image; however other participants only need to check whether or not the key image has been used before. If a malicious user attempts to spend the same output twice, it generates the same key image both times, and the network instantly rejects the fraudulent second transaction. Thanks to key images, the network can prevent output reuse, despite not knowing which outputs are spent!

The Monero network originally did not mandate ring signatures, which unfortunately allowed privacy-damaging *zero-mixin* transactions with no decoys. These early transactions had the same structure and weaknesses as transparent blockchains, by unequivocally identifying both the sender and receiver, along with revealing when the output is spent. Starting in 2016, the network began requiring two ring members for each signature, enforcing privacy-by-default for the sender. This was raised to a minimum *ring size* of five plausible signers in late 2017, and increased again to a minimum of seven potential signers in early 2018.

Note that between 2016 and 2018, ring size policies were formulated as a minimum number of mix-ins, and users were allowed to create transactions with larger rings if they desired. On paper, one

Figure 3.4 - Each Monero transaction is authorized by a group "ring signature," to protect the privacy of the sender.

might think that using more decoys in a transaction guarantees more privacy. However, there is a practical issue to take into consideration - when the vast majority of transactions use the minimum ring size, larger custom ring sizes stand out as unusual, which is counterproductive for privacy.

This was addressed in the late 2018 network upgrade; instead of specifying a minimum ring size, network policies now mandate a fixed ring size. At the time of writing, all transactions must use ring signatures with exactly eleven members. This number may increase in the future, as research into statistical threat models and best privacy practices continues to evolve.

3.2.4 Kovri

Kovri is a Monero feature created to protect a transaction's sender by concealing their IP address and physical location. Any device connected to the internet is assigned an IP address as an identifier to help route traffic to the correct user. However, this IP address can easily be connected to a user's physical location and personal identity.

The ability to link Monero activity and transactions to IP addresses has several significant downsides. Some of the cryptographic measures described in the previous section to protect Monero users may be partially circumvented if the IP addresses from node connection logs are analyzed to identify Monero users.

It is worth considering the unfortunate consequences that can arise when Monero network activity is connected to physical location and identity. Since broadcasting to the Monero network reveals an IP address, whichever node receives the transaction may be able to identify the physical location of the sender. While Monero's other privacy features make it difficult to link transactions from blockchain data alone, a surveilling node that observes multiple transactions originating from the same IP address could infer that they may be connected.

In addition to these privacy concerns, exposed IP addresses also enable potential censorship. A malicious node might choose to not relay transactions from certain individuals or groups. Even worse, the geographic information revealed by IP addresses might lead adversaries to pay a malicious visit to cryptocurrency users' doorsteps.

The connection between IP addresses and Monero activity is not only a threat for the users broadcasting transactions. The network traffic through nodes is currently visible to internet service providers and other surveilling parties, which could put node owners at risk if their government or internet service provider chooses to respond negatively toward cryptocurrencies.

Cryptocurrency miners may also experience unfair treatment if their IP addresses are linked to their network activity. Malicious parties might attack certain miners by censoring their blocks, perhaps due to some ideological disagreement, or to limit non-government or non-corporate mining.

Clearly, all parties in the Monero ecosystem benefit from the decoupling of their network activity from their IP addresses (and thus their physical location/identity). This type of anonymity is provided by Kovri, which is a routing technology designed to obscure transmissions' sources. It is based on the decentralized Invisible Internet Project (I2P) open specifications, which uses encryption and sophisticated routing techniques to create a private network distributed across the internet.

The Monero community is developing this lightweight security-focused software with a general open-source implementation and common APIs, so that it can also be used for other applications. Since Kovri is a peer-to-peer technology, all cryptocurrencies and services using the Kovri network benefit from increased adoption!

Kovri will soon be included with Monero releases, and will ultimately be enforced for all transactions as part of Monero's privacy-by-default policy.

If you have any questions, or would like to improve or implement Kovri, you can contact the lead developer (anonimal) on the Kovri

IRC channels #kovri, #kovri-dev, or his twitter account.

Figure 3.5 - Kovri creates a private relay network, to ensure that a user's Monero activity cannot be linked to their IP address or physical location.

3.3 Concluding comments

Monero uses several unique privacy technologies to protect various elements of the network and all parties in all transactions. RingCT conceals the amount sent in each transaction. Ring signatures protect the sender by concealing the source of the funds, while stealth addresses ensure that the recipient's address is not recorded on the blockchain. Kovri is an upcoming routing technology that breaks the link between your Monero activity, and your physical location/ identity.

Together, these features ensure that Monero users remain anonymous, and that funds are not trackable. By cryptographically eliminating all the links used in analyzing transactions on the blockchain, Monero achieves *fungibility*, which is a necessary characteristic of practical currencies. Now that you have read this chapter, you can understand how Monero protects the individuals described in the use cases described in chapter 1.

## Chapter 4

The Monero network

In this chapter, you'll learn the key concepts behind blockchain technology and how Monero miners keep the ledger secure. We'll begin by explaining the structure of *blocks*, the way that they're linked into a tamper-proof *chain*, and how the miners use *proof of work* to arrive at *consensus* on an agreed version of the ledger. On the topic of miners, we'll discuss the source of new moneroj, and how the coins are released into the ecosystem. Toward the end of the chapter, we'll dip our toes into a few cryptography concepts (*hashes* and *nonces*) to really grasp the actual process of mining.

4.1 The simplified anatomy of a block

The previous chapter discussed how transactions are constructed. In summary, your wallet drafts a message with instructions to transfer one of your outputs to a new recipient. Sensitive information in the message (sender, receiver, amount) is cryptographically obscured, before your wallet authorizes the message by digitally signing it with your private key.

In this chapter, you'll learn how the transaction message is processed to enact the actual transfer. When your wallet broadcasts this message, the network temporarily stores the request in a list of pending transactions known as the *memory pool*. The Monero miners collect these unconfirmed transactions from the memory pool, and bundle them together into *blocks*. A simplified block is shown on next page:

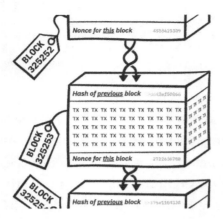

Figure 4.1 - Each sequentially-numbered block of transactions must include both a nonce and a reference to the hash of the previous block.

Each block contains a set of transactions, a cryptographic link to the previous block (called a *hash*), and a place for the miner to include a special number that completes the block (called a *nonce*).

If you want to learn how hashes and nonces work, there is a friendly introduction with examples toward the end of this chapter (you can skip ahead to the last section of chapter 4, and read it now if you're curious about the cryptography.) There are only two concepts that you need to know in order to understand how these techniques function to secure the blockchain:

1.   The *hash* is a security feature proving that each block is directly linked to an **unaltered** version of the previous block. If an attacker tries to tamper with any point in the ledger, even the smallest modification attempt will be blatantly obvious because the hashes will raise a red flag on every subsequent block.

2.   The *nonce* is a special string that completes the block and marks it as prepared for the blockchain. It is extremely computationally difficult to find a nonce that satisfies the requirements necessary to finalize and seal a block. Miners spend most of their time and energy searching for valid nonces. It is impossible to plan ahead

for calculating the nonces, so the search must start from scratch with each new block. Nonces are not mathematically meaningful; only one-time strings of random characters.

4.2 Nodes are the network backbone

4.2.1 Nodes relay network data to peers

Until now, references to "the Monero network" have mostly glossed over the details of its composition. How do your transactions actually propagate across this nebulous "network" to miners and other users? Thousands of Monero nodes scattered across the planet are connected to each other, quickly sharing news of transactions and blocks.

These nodes form a peer-to-peer network, enabling efficient and resilient communication for Monero users. Running a node does not require any special equipment or expertise - if you download and begin installing the Monero software now, you can have your own node running before you finish reading this chapter!

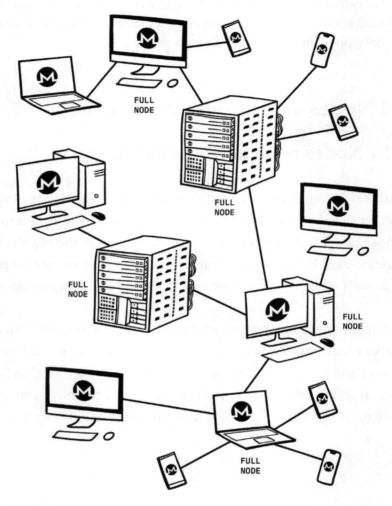

Figure 4.2 - Monero uses a distributed peer-to-peer network, comprised of a web of volunteer devices sharing new data with each other. Nodes retain a full copy of the blockchain and create the backbone of the network. Since running a node requires significant disk space, some devices (especially mobile wallets) instead connect to a remote node to request information and broadcast transactions.

There are no "special" or "super" nodes in Monero's peer-to-peer network; all nodes (including yours) are equal participants working to share resources and the workload. Nodes are hosted on computers of all shapes and sizes - laptops, desktops, servers, and even virtual machines.

4.2.2 Nodes store the blockchain

When a new node is initialized, it must first download the entire blockchain and verify the cryptographic links, such as the hashes and nonces. This initial sync may take a few hours, as the node builds its local copy of the blockchain, while confirming the validity of each transaction and block. Instead of downloading the blockchain over a single connection to a central source, each node receives transmissions from many peer nodes. Nodes do not need to identify or trust their peers, since the validity of the data is confirmed cryptographically.

Any Monero wallet software (e.g. the Monero GUI, a phone app, etc) must have access to a copy of the blockchain in order to carry out key tasks like retrieving transaction history, calculating account balances, and crafting transactions. A wallet cannot craft transactions before communicating with a synchronized node, since the software needs to find and tally the relevant unspent outputs. However, your address can receive moneroj whether or not you are connected to a synced node (it simply won't show up in your balance until the wallet downloads & verifies that block).

4.2.3 "Local nodes" versus "remote nodes"

The process of locally storing/verifying the entire blockchain so that your wallet can interact with your own copy of the ledger is referred to as running a *local node*. When you use this type of setup, your wallet only interacts with your personal copy of the blockchain. Running a local node requires a fair amount of disk space (~60 GB at the time of writing), which is not suitable for all devices, such as cell phones.

Thankfully, wallet software can be configured to use a *remote node* instead of your own local node. This means that your wallet will connect to somebody else's node and simply request information about your outputs. Most mobile Monero wallets default to using a remote node, in order to keep the app lightweight. The Monero GUI and CLI wallets can be configured to use either a local node or remote node.

There are no security risks in using a remote node; your seed and keys are never revealed, so the remote node operator will not be able to control your funds or decrypt any information that is protected by Monero features such as RingCT (concealing transaction amount) or stealth addresses (obfuscating recipient address).

There are some minor privacy concessions that come into play when using remote nodes, since the node operator is aware of the times and IP addresses from which your device broadcasts transactions or connects for updates. The upcoming Kovri privacy technology will significantly mitigate these risks. If you use your own local node, your wallet scans your personal copy of the blockchain for your transaction history, instead of relying on a third party to retrieve this information.

4.3 Miners create new blocks

4.3.1 Miners add new blocks onto the longest chain

The miners collect pending transactions from the memory pool, verify their authenticity by checking that the cryptographic proofs and signatures are valid, and check that the key image has not been used before (see "3.2.3 Ring signatures," to review why this is important).

To prepare a block, the miner drafts a list of transactions to be included, along with the hash of the previous block to provide a cryptographic link. Lastly, the miner labors to find a nonce that can be used to complete the block.

At any given moment, there are thousands of miners all working separately (or in teams, known as *mining pools*) to find a nonce that completes the current block of transactions. As soon as a miner or pool finds a nonce to finalize their block, they announce their version to the rest of the network. Upon receiving this completed block, the other miners and nodes append it to their copy of the blockchain, increasing the chain's *height* by one block. Transactions referenced by the new block are removed from the memory pool, and the other miners discard their own (incomplete) work on that block to begin preparing the next one.

4.3.2 A difficult task ensures stability and fairness

The global nature of the Monero ecosystem and unpredictable transmission delays due to network latency occasionally cause momentary splits in the blockchain, if two miners independently complete two different versions of a block at the same height. Suppose a miner in South America is the first to complete a block, but a different miner in Europe finishes their own copy before receiving the broadcast from South America. In this case, the western hemisphere may be temporarily using a different blockchain than the eastern hemisphere. For a brief moment, there exist two competing Monero ledgers that might have slight differences (depending on which pending transactions each miner selected from the memory pool). One might think that this would be a catastrophic occurrence!

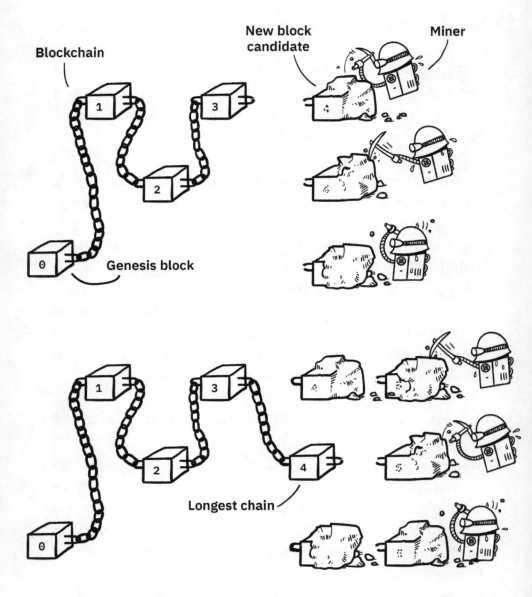

Figure 4.3 - Miners compete to extend the chain with a new block.
(Top) The blockchain is at height "3" so each miner works on their version of block "4".
(Bottom) Block "4" was completed by the middle miner first, so their version is added to the shared blockchain, and all miners switch to finding a nonce for block "5".

On the contrary, this situation is easily resolved by elegantly imposing a simple rule: miners all agree to work on the mining the next block in the **longest** chain. This is a key piece of Monero's *decentralized consensus* protocol, and allows the Monero network to nimbly reunite to a single chain after an accidental split. Instead of trying to resolve the discrepant blocks immediately, the miners simply continue working on completing the next block for their version.

Within the next few minutes, one of the miners will solve a subsequent block and add it to their chain. As soon as this occurs, their version becomes the longest chain, so the other miners and nodes quickly adopt that copy and discard the alternative *orphaned* block. Any transactions that were only included the orphaned block remain in the memory pool for the main chain, and will be mined in a subsequent block. By simply following the longest chain created with the most effort, the network completely resolves any splits and returns to consensus on a single universal ledger.

4.3.3 Monero "taxis" use a hard puzzle to ensure fairness

Validating a set of transactions and listing them in a block is not computationally difficult. The time-consuming task for the miner is finding a nonce that allows them to complete the block. This is a puzzle designed to be extremely challenging and solvable only by brute force testing solutions; there is no way to shortcut the process or mathematically narrow down the search for a valid nonce. Miners simply pick random numbers and test whether they complete the block, by trial and error.

The presence of this arbitrary obstacle may seem peculiar at first!

The miners carry out a crucial and computationally-easy role for the network (validating transactions) but are required to carry out a useless difficult task (finding the nonce) in order to submit their results.

To understand the reasoning behind this, consider the hypothetical **Monero Taxicab Network** with only a few vehicles, and many taxi drivers that can temporarily utilize one of the cabs if they submit an approved route. Throughout the day, potential riders call in and request rides all over the city. All of the requests from riders who have not been picked up are collected in a real-time "pool" of pending rides.

Figure 4.4 - In the first stage of preparing a ride plan, each driver looks at the pool of pending rides and drafts up a route.

Instead of a central taxi authority assigning each incoming ride to a car or driver, each taxi driver looks at the pool and puts together their own list of 5 - 10 trips that they could complete in the next 30 minutes. This part of route/ride planning is easy and fast for experienced taxi drivers! Once a driver puts together a list of trips that they can include in their next "*block*" of rides, they complete a final task described below, then submit their route to the Monero Taxicab Network.

If the driver has proposed a valid route with real pending riders, then the plan is approved! The riders included on the taxi driver's plan are removed from the pending pool, the taxi driver checks out a vehicle, and travelers are soon shuttled to their destinations. The driver collects fare from each of the riders, and receives a cash bonus from the Monero Taxicab Network for being the first to submit a complete plan.

So far, this should seem fairly intuitive! Incomplete trips are listed in a pool; when a taxi driver successfully submits an approved block of trips, the riders are transported to their destinations and removed from the pending pool.

Figure 4.5 - After the drivers complete the (relatively) easy task of planning a route, they must solve a difficult puzzle - in this analogy, finding a way to rearrange letters from the addresses to create a sentence.

However, the Monero Taxicab Network has a very peculiar rule: in order for a driver to submit their plan for a block of rides to the Monero Network, they must do some difficult useless task first. Imagine that the driver must scramble all of the letters in the riders' destination addresses and use some of them to generate five sentences (> 50 words total) that can say anything, but must have correct grammar/spelling in the local language. A driver submitting a planned route must include both the list of rides and the nonsense ("*nonce*") sentences that match the letters in the destinations, or else their route will be automatically rejected. There are multiple valid nonce phrases that can be constructed from most sets of letters (for example {a,e,e,g,i,m,n,r,r,s,t,o,o} can be rearranged to form both "Rims enrage too!" and "Monero is great!"), and the resulting sentences are absolutely useless for anything besides submitting that set of rides to the Monero Taxicab Network.

A property of this type of task, which will have parallels in the Monero cryptocurrency, is that it is **very hard to find** a nonce, and **very easy to verify one.** For this taxi scenario, is quite difficult to rearrange a dozen addresses by hand into 50 words that form valid sentences. However, it is trivial for somebody else to review the nonce result and verify that it completes the block of rides. When a driver submits their nonce in the format shown below, you can very quickly confirm that "Apple jam is very bad" is a valid sentence, and that the letters are properly constructed from the rider destinations. This verification is nearly instantaneous, compared to the time it took the driver to rearrange the letters and find several sentences.

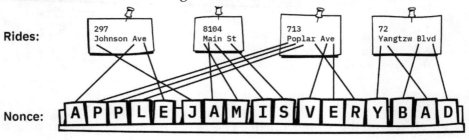

Figure 4.6 - Finding a nonce sentence by rearranging the addresses is tricky and time-consuming. However, the validity of a submission is easy to verify by quickly checking that it only uses letters from the rides included in the route.

A seasoned taxi driver would be able to plan the driving route from the trip list in less than 60 seconds, however it will probably take them a few minutes to rearrange the letters and find nonce sentences by hand. In fact, most of their effort in preparing their proposed block of rides will be spent on finding this useless nonce.

Imagine this process from a taxi driver's perspective, beginning right after the last block was approved. You quickly create a route that includes several trips from the list of pending rides. Then you begin working furiously to rearrange letters from the destinations into some kind of nonce sentence. For a few minutes, you and all of the other taxi drivers are working on the same list of pending rides, each trying to craft a long enough nonce with more than 50 words. Suddenly, a different driver submits a list of the rides along with a completed nonce. All of the trips that you were working on disappear from the pool! You must throw away your work on that block (since the riders are already en route) and switch to a new set of pending trips. The process to find a valid nonce for that set of riders begins again from scratch, based on the new set of letters in their destinations.

Why would the Monero Taxicab Network impose such a difficult useless task upon their drivers? It is actually their surefire way to ensure that customers are served fairly! Imagine that a few of the taxi drivers behave unethically in some way, perhaps ignoring pending rides called in from a certain part of town, or selecting only the riders that are going to businesses that have bribed those unfair drivers. Without the nonce requirement, these small groups or individual malicious drivers might dominate the ride selection process for the whole business by constantly submitting their (unfair or exclusionary) routes as soon as a car becomes available. In this way, they could systematically treat some groups of customers poorly, which is absolutely antithetical to the core principles of the Monero Taxicab Network, which is dedicated to serving all riders fairly.

The nonce task competition between many taxi drivers is crucial to Monero's goal of ensuring that cars and rides are provided fairly. Assuming that all of the taxi drivers can rearrange letters at roughly the same speed as each other, it will be somewhat random which driver lucks into a solution and is able to submit their block of plans first. It is unlikely that any driver could be the first to submit multiple block plans in a row (i.e. be the first to find nonce sentences for several sequential blocks) since each driver is competing against, and collectively outnumbered by, all of the other drivers.

Most of the multitude of potential drivers will be honest individuals, submitting fair ride block plans to keep the city running smoothly. If there are a few malicious drivers who wish to submit unfair plans, the nonce task prevents them from controlling the entire system. Statistically, they will occasionally be the first to find the nonce, and thus able to submit their exclusionary route plan for that block. However, the rest of the drivers, most of whom are honest, will immediately begin working on their fair blocks to propose for the next set of rides! Due to the random nature of who lucks into finding a nonce first, the next set of rides will probably be carried out by an honest driver whose plan will incorporate the previously-excluded trips. This system of imposing useless work to randomize which drivers' routes are accepted allows the Monero Taxicab Network to be sure that a minority of malicious drivers cannot block a user or group from booking rides.

The Monero Taxicab Network thus has no central authority that is responsible or liable for controlling ride activity and assignment. Instead, this task is distributed to the individual drivers, employing the useless nonce competition to randomly select which route proposal is accepted. This statistically ensures that the cars are frequently assigned to honest drivers, so the Monero Taxicab Network has an excellent reputation for providing fair service to all customers.

By now you're probably wondering how this extended taxicab metaphor is related to the cryptocurrency that this book is ostensibly about! You might have figured out that the decentralized Monero Taxicab Network is an overt analogy for the Monero cryptocurrency network, which needs to provide fair global service without any central authority.

Each trip corresponds to a Monero transaction, pending in the memory pool until it is selected for a spot in a car/block. The taxi drivers represent miners. Both carry out an easy important jobs (taxi drivers plan routes; miners collect and validate transactions), yet are forced to compete against other drivers/miners in a useless difficult nonce task. This barrier randomizes who succeeds first - thus statistically distributing most of the cars/blocks to honest drivers/miners. Whichever taxi driver submits their route first is rewarded with a bonus from the Monero Taxicab Company and fare from each of the riders who obtained a spot. Likewise, miners are rewarded with a commission (called the *coinbase* or *block reward*) for completing each block, and they also collect fees from the transactions included in the block.

4.3.4 Miners are paid for their service

Each time a miner successfully mines a block (i.e. is the first to find a nonce that completes the next block on the longest chain) they are paid two different ways.

1. First, the miner receives a reward for contributing a completed block of validated transactions. This *block reward* is analogous to the cash bonus that the taxi network paid drivers that submitted

completed routes. All miners, upon receiving and confirming the solved block, add this freshly-minted *coinbase* to the address of the miner who found the valid nonce first.

2. Secondly, the miner collects fees that were included with the transactions. Monero users can increase the likelihood that a miner includes their transaction sooner by including a larger fee.

It is a common misconception that miners are "finding" or "creating" coins. Actually, miners are simply validating transactions, and are paid for their work with new coins. This introduction of new moneroj is referred to as *coin emission*.

When Monero was launched, the coin emission rate was more than 30 XMR every 2 minutes. This reward will smoothly decrease until it reaches 0.6 XMR per 2-minute block in 2022. Monero's continuous decrease is designed to provide a more stable economic environment for miners, compared to other cryptocurrencies' dramatic *halving* events, when the block reward is abruptly substantially reduced. After 2022, Monero's *tail emission* will stay constant, guaranteeing that mining a block will always reward 0.6 XMR.

Many cryptocurrencies have a fixed cap on coin emission, with a hard limit on maximum supply. Once the supply cap is reached, there will be no new coins introduced for miners, who will be forced to subsist entirely on fees. For example, in Bitcoin, this paradigm shift in financial incentives will occur around 2140, when the supply reaches 21 million Bitcoins and ceases to increase any further. This approach is often touted as a benefit to remain "deflationary," however these arguments are often based on conflating the concept of an inflating monetary supply with a different use of the word "inflation" to describe an undesirable decrease in spending power of a currency.

The annual supply increase from Monero's 0.6 XMR tail emission is less than 1% per year. Since the miners will always be able to collect fees, the guaranteed coinbase payments provide greater financial stability for the miners in the long run. This social contract ensures that the miners remain incentivized to use their equipment to secure the Monero network.

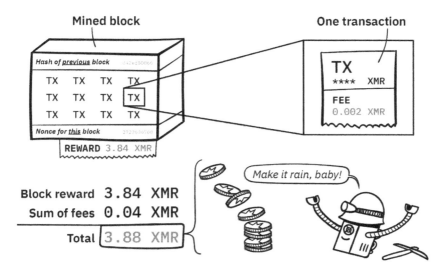

Figure 4.7 - A miner receives two types of payments each time they mine a block: 1) the fees included with each transaction, and 2) a block reward consisting of freshly-minted moneroj.

4.4 Proof of Work systems

Now we'll step away from the taxi analogy and directly discuss the systems in place to ensure fairness in Monero. This process of coupling important network functions with the search for a useless nonce is referred to as a *Proof of Work* system. Many cryptocurrencies are built on PoW-based consensus, and there are differences among various implementations with different characteristics. However, they share a common theme of enforcing decentralization by requiring validation to be submitted with a nonce. Sometimes the nonce itself is referred to as the "proof of work," referring to the piece of data that was hard to find/create and easy to verify, such as the taxi drivers' anagrams.

Miners measure how quickly they can work toward mining blocks in "hashes per second", abbreviated H/s. Each miner can measure their *hashrate*, which varies depending on the equipment that they are using to mine. The *"network hashrate"* refers to the total hashrate of all the miners working on preparing blocks.

4.4.1 Benefits

4.4.1.1 Censorship resistance

In PoW systems, the nonce-finding competition described above randomizes which miner's version is accepted as the latest block on the longest chain. As mentioned in the taxi analogy, the PoW framework prevents effective censorship. Some malicious miner in the Monero network may try to provide preferential treatment or exclude certain transactions in the memory pool, however an honest Monero miner will simply include those transactions in the next block.

4.4.1.2 Double-spend attack prevention

There is another blockchain challenge solved by PoW systems that was not included in the taxi analogy. Specifically, a malicious miner might try to *double spend* an output. This refers to an attack where the miner creates alternative blocks to undo their past transactions and steal back the money for themselves. The attack would have to proceed in this manner:

- Malicious miner Martin broadcasts a transaction sending some of his moneroj to victim "Valerie".
- When the "Martin >> Valerie" transaction is mined onto the blockchain, Valerie believes she has been paid.
- Martin takes whatever he was buying from Valerie...
- ... then Martin mines a different version of the block that originally contained the Martin >> Valerie transaction.
- In Martin's alternative version, the transaction to Valerie doesn't exist! Instead, his second version contains a transaction that sends that moneroj to one of his wallets (Martin >> Martin), instead of Valerie's.
- If Martin can quickly mine enough blocks to make his chain the longest, then the network will accept his alternate reality. In practice, the infeasibility of this step prevents double-spend attacks from occurring.
- Since the key image for Martin's output appears on the chain (now associated with the transaction to himself), the network will no longer accept the "Martin >> Valerie" transaction as valid since the key image associated with that output is already spent.

At this point, Martin has left with whatever he bought from Valerie and has also stolen back the moneroj that he initially used to pay her.

Thankfully, PoW systems prevent an attacker from sustaining this type of double-spend attack, by limiting the speed with which they can generate blocks. Recall that miners will always follow the longest blockchain, so the malicious miner would have to change the block with the previous transaction then re-mine every block afterward, fast enough to overtake the length of the main chain. Since the malicious miner will be working alone to generate the altered blocks, against the hashrate of the entire rest of the network maintaining the original ledger, the attacker will be unable to catch up. This type of attack could only feasibly succeed if the malicious miner has as much computing power as the entire rest of the network combined. For this reason, the term *51% attack* is often used to indicate that some sort of malicious activity would require majority hashrate.

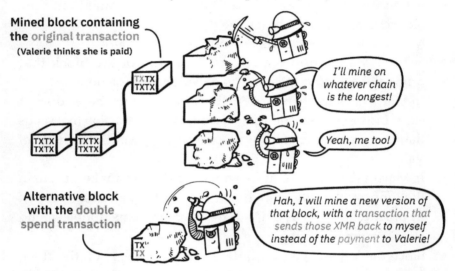

Figure 4.8.a - The dishonest miner at the bottom attempts a double-spend attack by creating a different version of an already-mined block.

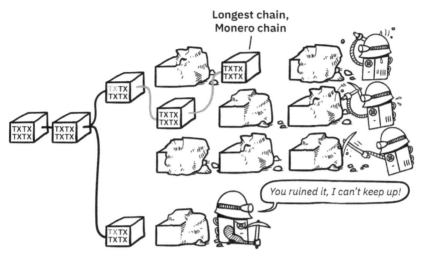

Longest chain,
Monero chain

You ruined it, I can't keep up!

Figure 4.8.b - All of the honest miners working together produce blocks faster than the malicious miner, so the attacker's chain with the alternative transaction is discarded.

A cryptocurrency with more miners and a greater total network hashrate will be more difficult to attack in this way, since the malicious miner must have more computing power than the rest of the global network. Increasing the total hashrate by including more miners helps to secure the network against attacks.

4.4.2 The "difficulty" adjusts time between blocks

The Monero network aims to add a new block onto the chain approximately every two minutes. With each mined block, some transactions are moved from the pending memory pool onto the confirmed blockchain. If the average blocktime becomes too long, transactions will be too slow to confirm. If the average blocktime is too short, then the network could get out of sync more often.

The network influences how quickly blocks are mined by adjusting the *difficulty* of the nonce puzzle. As more miners join the network over time, their collective guessing power (hashrate) results in blocks being completed more frequently (conceptually: if you double the number of people searching for something, the group will probably find it in half the time). This would statistically cause miners to find blocks faster than the target blocktime of 2 minutes. To compensate for this, the difficulty of the puzzle is increased, meaning that it takes longer to find a nonce that matches the arbitrary requirements. Likewise, the difficulty can be adjusted to be easier if mining power decreases, causing blocks to be completed too infrequently.

In the taxi network analogy from the previous section, the difficulty of the letter rearrangement task could be similarly arbitrarily adjusted by requiring more or fewer words in the nonce sentences. If 20% of the taxi drivers (miners) did not participate one day, then it would take longer on average for route plan blocks (completed with nonces) to be submitted, so some cars would be idling with no driver. To correct this, the taxi drivers would agree to lower the nonce requirements from 50 words to 40 words. This would put the drivers back in sync with the availability of cars.

Difficulty increases proportionally with total network hashrate to keep the flow of blocks constant.

4.4.3 The CryptoNight algorithm

Monero uses a variation of the CryptoNight PoW algorithm, which is significantly different than the systems used by most other cryptocurrencies. One of Monero's defining features is its use of a PoW function that is difficult to optimize for specialized mining equipment.

In most contexts, 'optimization' is a good thing, so you might be surprised that Monero's PoW algorithm intentionally stymies accelerating mining speeds. This is because the ability to create overpowered

94

mining equipment can lead to a dangerous centralization of miners. These risks are perfectly illustrated in the history of Bitcoin mining.

4.4.3.1 Context: The history of Bitcoin mining

When cryptocurrencies entered the scene with Bitcoin's appearance in 2009, mining occurred exclusively on computer CPUs. Since the network mining difficulty adjusts to the current total hashrate, CPU mining was adequately profitable in the early days. CPU miners have Bitcoin hashing power on the order of 1,000,000 H/s, written as 1 MH/s for convenience.

Soon, graphics cards were repurposed for mining cryptocurrencies. GPUs are able to attack the mining problem orders of magnitude faster, around 100 MH/s. Since the network difficulty adjusted based on the GPU miners, the CPU miners could not compete (i.e. mining rewards were insufficient to pay for the equipment and electricity costs).

Next, application-specific integrated circuits (ASICs) were built for the sole purpose of mining Bitcoin. These special devices are quite expensive, and mine many thousands of times faster than GPUs - more than 1,000,000 MH/s. By now, the Bitcoin network difficulty has increased to accommodate the ASICs, consequently pushing the CPU and GPU miners out of business.

Bitcoin was initially launched with the vision that anybody in the world with a computer could begin mining to secure the network and obtain some bitcoins as a reward. Unfortunately, the creation and proliferation of ASICs very effectively ended this dream. If you wish to begin mining Bitcoin now, you will have to obtain an ASIC for hundreds or thousands of Euros.

This ASIC takeover put the vast majority of Bitcoin miners out of business. The network began its existence secured by scores of computer geeks scattered across the globe, all participating on their personal computers and graphics cards. Sadly, this true decentralization of Bitcoin is a bygone era. Now the network is dominated by several large corporations with massive ASIC farms, who have effectively become the Bitcoin backbone.

4.4.3.2 ASICs enable dangerous centralization

Since many of the main cryptocurrencies are dominated by ASIC miners, it is worth giving consideration to the topic and its risks. Centralization occurs in two forms: ASICs are only produced by a few companies (centralization of manufacturing) and subsequent mining tends to be limited to a few large farms (centralization of mining).

Centralization of ASIC manufacturing and mining to a few large corporations allows hackers, attackers, and governments to exert disproportionately large influence over the network and its operation. This begins to nullify many of the benefits of decentralization. For example:

- **Universal access to mining** flourished in the days of CPU and GPU mining, which uses mostly unregulated general-purpose hardware. However, mining now requires specialized hardware, which is at much greater risk of targed regulation and control. It is possible that some government may impose bans or require licenses to manufacture/own ASICs.

- **Censorship resistance** is weakened if the majority of Monero's hash power is controlled by large mining farms that can be pressured into confirming or censoring certain transactions.

It would be difficult to exert this influence over a global collection of ameteur miners, and much easier to impose this kind of activity on centralized mining corporations.

- **Network resilience** may be catastrophically undermined if a malicious manufacturer (or one that is following government orders) includes an secret ASIC killswitch to remotely control or shut down their mining equipment. This creates a single point of failure, whose activation would instantly kill most of the network hashrate. This would plunge the network into a sudden vulnerable state with dramatically lessened hashrate to secure the currency. This risk is much higher if a small number of ASIC manufacters control the majority of production.

The ASIC takeover of Bitcoin is complete. While there are still some small-time miners with ASICS working in pools, large mining farms dominate the network hashrate. Concerningly, the majority of Bitcoin ASICs are designed, manufactured, and shipped by a single manufacturer - in stark contrast to the Bitcoin's early days, when miners used every brand, model, and flavor of CPU and GPU to mine. The prevalence of ASICs would be much less risky if there was a diverse and competitive ASIC market.

4.4.3.3 Monero actively resists ASICs

Due to underlying egalitarian principles, the Monero community does not approve of ASICs and their inevitable centralization of mining power. While the "CPU-hard" hash algorithm (SHA-256) used by Bitcoin is amenable to ASIC optimization, Monero deters ASIC development by using a "memory-hard" algorithm (CryptoNight) that is difficult to accelerate.

Consequently, CPU and GPU mining are both feasible for Monero, even in 2018. There are currently billions of existing devices (any modern x86 CPU and many GPUs) that are capable of mining Monero, so the process is accessible to any internet-connected individual. In fact, it is even possible to mine Monero in a web browser from any phone or computer!

In early March 2018, the Monero community was shocked to realize that CryptoNight ASICs had been secretly produced and were mining Monero! These devices purported to mine Monero 25 times faster than the leading GPUs, and retrospective hashrate analysis suggests that they accounted for nearly half of the Monero network hashrate in late 2017 and early 2018.

Since the CryptoNight algorithm was designed as a memory-hard function specifically to "close the gap between CPU (majority) and GPU/FPGA/ASIC (minority) miners," the existence of these ASICs was an unexpected discovery. While the CryptoNote authors observe that, "It is appropriate that some users can have a certain advantage over others," they propose that "their investments should grow at least linearly with the power." Naturally, a newer computer or a nicer graphics card will mine more efficiently than older equipment, but ASICs create an extremely disproportionate distribution of hashrate.

The Monero community reacted quickly, proactively taking steps to mitigate ASIC mining before the existence of the devices was even fully confirmed. The spring 2018 Monero routine upgrade included a minor tweak to the CryptoNight algorithm, designed to affect ASICs differently than GPU/CPU miners. This slight variation did not change the difficulty or behavior of the algorithm, so the CPU/GPU miners were able to easily adjust to the new variant when they upgraded with the network.

ASICs, on the other hand, are fundamentally incapable of adapting to new (minor or major) variations. One can think of ASICs as workers that are trained to do one task extremely quickly, but cannot learn to do anything else. The algorithm to be executed is physically etched into the ASIC circuits, so they cannot be reprogrammed or repurposed.

When the minor CryptoNote tweak was implemented at block 1546000, the ASICs became instantly incompatible with the network, and approximately half of the total hashrate vanished. Since the ASICs were unable to adjust to process blocks by a modified algorithm, any blocks they produce are now immediately rejected by the Monero network as invalid.

For the time being, it appears that the Monero network has successfully mitigated the unexpected ASIC threat. To permanently discourage ASICs, Monero now slightly changes the mining algorithm at each network update. Since Monero carries out routine hard forks every 6 months, this should permanently disincentivize attempts to produce Monero ASICs, since each expensive and lengthy redesign would be promptly rendered obsolete.

4.4.4 Brief note on PoW alternatives

There are alternative systems for maintaining fairness besides proof of work; examples include proof of stake, proof of space, proof of bandwidth, and even hybrids between multiple types. Each system has its own strengths and drawbacks. PoW is currently the most widely used and field-tested consensus mechanism, and is currently the only system utilized by Monero.

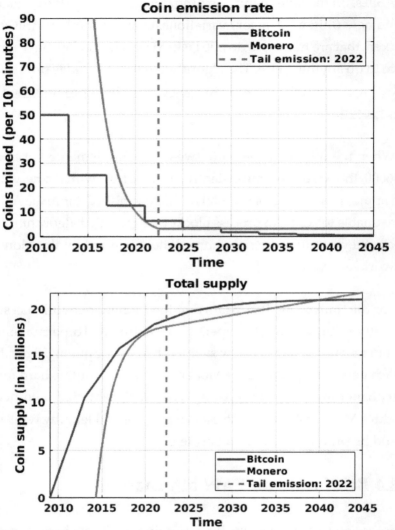

Figure 4.9 -Visualization of differences between the Bitcoin (blue) and Monero (red) monetary supply policies. The dashed red vertical line shows when Monero transitions to a fixed tail emission in 2022.

The top panel shows the coin emission rate (per 10 minutes, to take into account the different block times). Bitcoin reduces coinbase amounts through 'halving events, whereas Monero smoothly decreases the block reward until tail emission activates.

The bottom panel shows the total coin supply. The Bitcoin coin supply asymptotically approaches 21 million BTC in 2140, while the Monero supply increases at a fixed rate.

4.5 Cryptographic concepts for proof of work

Throughout this chapter, we've focused on the functionality of hashes and nonces, describing them primarily through analogies. If you want to learn how they really work, the remainder of the chapter introduces the actual cryptographic principles.

4.5.1 Hashes (general concept)

Hash functions are a cryptographic tool that can digest any input data, and produce a unique fingerprint output. These algorithms are designed so that any alteration to the input, even very minor changes, will result in an entirely different output. The term "hash" can be used to refer to both the function itself and its output for a particular input.

Adding, removing, or changing even a single character will result in a totally different hash. Consider the message "`Please send 50 euros to Jen.`" We can run the string through one of these algorithms to produce its hash `a2d2a9059ed8d323` The below table shows how the hash output changes dramatically with any modification of the input:

Input	Output hash	Comment
Please send 50 EUR to Jen.	a2d2a9059ed8d323	True message
Please send 500 EUR to Jen.	05cbdd8dd96718ac	Added an extra '0' to amount
Please send 60 EUR to Jen.	f5087a90b63b1777	Changed '5' to '6'

Input	Output hash	Comment
Please send 50 EUR to Jon.	ffd424b7077a3c58	Changed recipient to 'Jon'
Please send 50 EUR to Jen.	a2d2a9059ed8d323	Same input = same output!

the example output here is the first 16 characters of each input's SHA-256 hash
$ echo {input} | sha256sum | cut -c1-16

Hash functions are heavily utilized in many cryptocurrency security features. Cryptographic hash functions are engineered to be *collision-resistant,* which means that it is hard to find two input messages that *collide* to produce the same output digest. This is central to the immutability (tamperproof nature) of the blockchain, since any attempts to change data in a past block will result in an entirely different hash output for that and all subsequent blocks.

This notion of an expanding append-only database with each group of entries cryptographically secured by hashes to the previous block is a key concept behind the blockchain revolution.

4.5.2 Nonces (general concept)

The term *nonce* refers to a puzzle that is not inherently physically/ mathematically meaningful. For example, consider the following "fill-in-the-blank" questions that a teacher might give their students:

- Puzzle A) The Esperanto word for "c___" inspired the name "Monero". Acceptable **answer**: "coin"

- Puzzle B) 1 kilogram is equal to "_____" grams.
  Acceptable **answer**: 1000

- Puzzle C) This 3-digit prime number "3___" does not repeat any digits. Acceptable **nonces**: any of {307, 317, 347, 349, 359, etc...}

- Puzzle D) This 5-digit prime number "7___" does not repeat any digits. Acceptable **nonces**: any of {71263, 72169, 73609, 74869, etc...}

Puzzle A and B are both meaningful, and each have one correct answer (A: "coin" B: "1000") that the student will want to remember for future problems. Thus, these answers are not considered "nonces".

However, puzzles C and D are both "busy work" tasks that are hard to solve, and do not contribute insight to any real problem. There are multiple solutions that all satisfy the nonce requirement; for question C, the answer "359" is equally as valid as "307."

A student that spends an hour testing various numbers to come up with the answer "359" for puzzle C has to start the search for a valid nonce from scratch upon encountering each variation on the puzzle, e.g. *"This 3-digit prime number "6___" does not repeat any digits."*

If you only had a pencil and paper (or even with a calculator), would you rather solve puzzle C or puzzle D? Probably puzzle C, since you're likely to find a valid 3-digit answer faster than a valid 5-digit answer. You can see how the difficulty of the problem can be arbitrarily adjusted by changing how many digits are required.

4.6 PoW concept summary

Cryptocurrencies use the hash of each block to ensure that its contents have not been changed, since modifying a single character would be instantly obvious due to the radically-different hash (which propagates through subsequent blocks). The hash of a block includes all of its contents: transactions, headers, the hash of the previous block, and a nonce field.

To work on completing a block, the miners must randomly guess at values for the nonce, attempting to find one that causes the hash of the entire block to produce an output below a certain threshold, which is determined by the current network difficulty. Since it is impossible to predict how changing the inputs to a hash function will affect its outputs, the miners must brute force random nonces by trial and error until they find one that produces an output hash that satisfies the current network difficulty.

The network raises or lowers this threshold to influence the mining difficulty, in order to maintain a 2-minute block time independent of changes in the total hashrate.

## Chapter 5

A deep dive into Monero & cryptography

Since long before the birth of computers, mathematics and cryptography have been at the center of communication and information exchange. While simple ciphers have been around since Caesar's time, modern cryptography was born during the World Wars for encrypting important and confidential messages. Initially, governments and militaries funded classified cryptography research to identify protocols for protecting state secrets.

Now, cryptography is no longer limited to spies and militaries; it forms the backbone of communication and security in the internet era, and is widely studied by academic and industry researchers scattered across the globe.

Today, cryptography is a ubiquitous behind-the-scenes tool that enables security, management, communication, and many of the connections that improve our day-to-day lives. For example, consider the invention of Secure Socket Layer (SSL, deprecated in favor of TSL), which is based on cryptographically signing the content. Hospitals, banks, governments, and businesses all protect your data with cryptography.

This chapter discusses how cryptographic tools can be applied to a decentralized financial database to give rise to cryptocurrencies, especially Monero.

5.1 Math fundamentals

Here is a brief introduction/recap of several mathematical principles that are at the core of cryptography.

5.1.1 Euclidean division (A/B)

Dividing any number A by another B, written as A/B or A÷B returns an answer that can either be written as a quotient with a remainder, or as a decimal alone.

Generally:

A/B = q with remainder r

$$\frac{a}{b}$$

For example:

12/4 = 3 with remainder 0, which can be written 3.0 in decimal form

13/4 = 3 with remainder 1, which can be written 3.25 in decimal form

27/5 = 5 with remainder 2, which can be written 5.4 in decimal form

5.1.2 Prime numbers

A prime number is any integer (whole number) that is not divisible by any integer besides '1' and itself. For example:

20 is not prime because it is divisible by 2, 4, 5, and 10, resulting in whole numbers

e.g. $20 \div 4 = 5$

- or -

$20 \div 10 = 2$

7 is prime because any integer that you divide it by will not yield a whole number

  e.g. $7 \div 3 = 2.3333$

Some example prime numbers include 3, 5, 7, 11, 13, 97, 223, 997, 3413, 4421, 17837, 145601, 428567, 1171967, and even much larger numbers like 2074722246773485207821695222107608587480 9964747 2111729275299258991219668475054965831008441 6732550077 or the twin primes $2{,}996{,}863{,}034{,}895 \times 2^{1{,}290{,}000} \pm 1$, which have over 350,000 digits each!

5.1.3 Modular arithmetic

Modular arithmetic describes numbers that wrap around a particular integer. An intuitive example is the 12-hour clock. If you stay up for 5 hours past 11:00 PM, you would not encounter 16:00 PM o'clock! Instead, at midnight, the time wraps around to zero (so 5 hours past 11:00 PM is 4:00 AM the next day).

Given any two positive numbers, A (the dividend) and B (the divisor),

`A modulo B =` the remainder r from A/B.

In the context of clocks, staying up 5 hours past 11:00 PM could be represented as:

(11:00 PM + 5 hours) mod 12 = …

  = 16:00 mod 12

  = 4:00 (AM)

5.1.4 Integer representation

Integers can be represented in many different encodings, several of which are encountered frequently in computer science.

Most people are quite familiar with the base-10 "decimal" system, which represents numbers using 10 characters:
0,1,2,3,4,5,6,7,8,9.

"Hex" encoding adds 6 extra characters, for a base-16 set:
0,1,2,3,4,5,6,7,8,9,a,b,c,d,e,f.

The integer written as 11719682 in base-10 can be expressed as B2D402 in base-16. Note that a larger character set requires fewer digits (shorter strings) to express the same number.

Computers "think" in base-2, using only the characters "0" and "1." This is called *binary* and the number 11719682 (base-10) would be represented as 101100101101010000000010.

Monero prints final addresses and keys in base-58, which uses Arabic numerals and most of the Latin character set (both uppercase and lowercase). It is similar to another scheme called Base64, however it has been modified to avoid numbers and letters that might look ambiguous when printed. Monero uses this format, strictly for the convenience of human users, who often must manually read or transcribe long addresses.

The base-58 alphabet is:

123456789ABCDEFGHJKLMNPQRSTUVWXYZ-
abcdefghijkmnopqrstuvwxyz

Note: Zero (0) along with the letters I (uppercase i), O (uppercase o), and l (lowercase L) are not present in this Base58 alphabet due to their ambiguity with each other.

5.1.5 Elliptic curves

5.1.5.1 General introduction

Elliptic curves are defined as the set of 2-dimensional (x, y) points that satisfy an equation:

$$y^2 = x^3 + ax + b.$$

For example, with fixed coefficients a = 2 and b = 3, this equation becomes

$$y^2 = x^3 + 2x + 3,$$

which is satisfied by many pairs of points such as:

x = 3 and y = 6
x = 3 and y = -6
x = -1 and y = 0.

5.1.5.2 Ed25519 Twisted Edwards

Monero uses a particular *Twisted Edwards* elliptic curve for cryptographic operations, Ed25519, which is the birational equivalent of the Montgomery curve Curve25519.

The ed25519 curve can be expressed algebraically as

$$- x^2 + y^2 = 1 - (121665/121666)\ x^2\ y^2.$$

Thinking back to our general elliptic curve equation, this Twisted Edwards is a special case using the parameters:

$$a = -1 \text{ and } b = 121665/121666.$$

Recently, it has become clear that a NIST-backed PRNG (Pseudo-random Number Generator Algorithm) is flawed, and contains a potential backdoor. Since the NIST4 standard algorithms have had recent issues, and the Twisted Edwards curve was selected to address many concerns held by the cryptography community.

Seen from a broader perspective, curves selected by the NIST are also implicitly supported by the NSA. These endorsements are viewed suspiciously by the cryptography and cryptocurrency communities due to previous incidents when the NSA used their authority over NIST to weaken algorithms suggested by the latter.

Twisted Edwards curve Ed25519 is not subject to any patents, and the team behind it has developed and adapted basic cryptographic algorithms with efficiency in mind. This curve is currently believed to be secure.

5.1.5.3 Elliptical operations

Elliptic curve point addition and scalar multiplication are fundamental operations for elliptic curve cryptography schemes. It's helpful to have a basic understanding of these concepts before we dive into the mechanics of Monero's calculations.

Elliptic curve point addition operates differently than the typical addition encountered in everyday arithmetic. To add two points together on an elliptic curve you must find the line between those two points and then find the point at which the curve intersects with that line. That point is then reflected over the x-axis to arrive at the final point.

When adding a point to itself, known as *point doubling*, you must find the tangent line to the starting point to get to the point at which that tangent line intersects with the curve. That point is then reflected over the x-axis to arrive at the final point.

Scalar multiplication utilizes both a point on the curve and an integer. To multiply a point, P, by an integer, S, the point is added to itself S times. Many cryptographic schemes, such as those employed by Monero, use a common base point on the elliptic curve as a generator point to generate public keys from private keys.

When the curve generator point is added to itself many times, the resulting point cannot be used to determine how many times the operation occurred. This problem is often referred to as the elliptic curve discrete logarithm problem. This kind of scalar multiplication is considered a one-way function, since reversing the operation is so difficult.

5.2 Cryptography basics

Monero is the leading secure and untraceable cryptocurrency thanks to its unique privacy-oriented cryptographic features, which we'll explore more thoroughly in this chapter. This is one of the more technical chapters of the book, due to the mathematical nature of cryptography. More complex techniques are built upon simple principles known as *cryptographic primitives*.

A cryptographic primitive is an algorithm that serves as the building block for cryptographic protocols. Monero employs a wide variety of cryptographic primitives for various uses, some of which we covered conceptually in chapters 3 and 4. Monero's intentional approaches to privacy and (ASIC-resistant) proof of work require more sophisticated cryptographic tools than those used by many other cryptocurrencies.

5.2.1 Symmetric and asymmetric cryptography

For encrypting data, algorithms can be characterized as *symmetric* or *asymmetric* depending on what type of keys are used.

Symmetric encryption requires the participants to share a secret, for example you encrypt a message by the password "hunter2" and the recipient uses the password "hunter2" to decrypt it. To communicate in this way, both parties must have agreed on the shared (symmetric) secret ahead of time. This practical issue limits the utility of symmetric encryption for many applications.

Asymmetric encryption allows two parties to interact securely without sharing a particular secret. This type of cryptography is woven into the framework of internet security, end-to-end messengers, and cryptocurrencies.

Bitcoin uses asymmetric encryption with two keys:

- private key - for signing transactions and for decrypting data
- public key - for signature verification and encrypting data

Monero's more complex cryptographic framework requires four keys:

- public view key - used to verify the validity of addresses
- private view key - used for viewing data such as the balance, fees and transactions amounts (the view key cannot create or sign transactions)
- public spend key - another public key for transaction verification
- private spend key - used for signing transactions, i.e. sending moneroj

Your public Monero address is a direct representations of the pair of public keys, whereas Bitcoin (and clones) use a hash of their single public key. EdDSA keys (both private and public) are 256 bits long, or 64 hexadecimal characters. Not every 256-bit integer is a valid EdDSA scalar (private key); it must be less than the "curve order" described with the equation in the Ed25519 function section.

5.2.2 Hashing

Chapter 4 discussed the concept of *hashing* and how its uses range from confirming data fidelity to distributing rewards in Proof of Work. Example hashes are shown in the cryptography section toward the end of Chapter 4.

Selecting a good hashing algorithm is crucial for generating addresses and keys in a secure way. If two different inputs produce the same hash output, this is known as a *collision*. Hashes are commonly used as an identifier in blockchain systems, relying on their effective uniqueness. Furthermore, a collision during seed generation would lead to multiple individuals with the same keys and addresses; obviously this would be extremely problematic!

Monero uses the CryptoNight PoW system, which employs a special *CryptoNote* hash algorithm, which is build on the *Keccak* hash. The Keccak algorithm won a NIST competition to be designated *SHA3*, and is designed by non-NSA engineers. Monero uses the *Keccak-256* hashing function with 32-byte output for both transaction and block hashing.

5.2.3 Monero pseudorandom number generation (PRNG)

When users and computers are creating new keys, it is crucial that they find new keys that others cannot guess. This is actually a very difficult task, since both hardware and software are typically designed to favor reproducibility. If the computer generates randomness in a predictable way, then the output can be ostensibly random but somewhat easier to guess.

For example consider a PRNG that simply shuffles the digits of the current time to make a 4-digit key. So at "10:34" it might output "0413" or "1403" or "0134" … If you wanted to keep the output key secret, this would be a terrible method for a few reasons:

- An attacker who knows that you made your key when you got to work around 12:45 AM would know that the digits "1" and "2" appear, which narrows the choices down to significantly fewer options.

- There are no HH:MM times of day with three "9"s. In fact, there are no times with any three digits chosen from {6,7,8,9} since 17:89 h, 18:78 h, etc are impossible times. This rule eliminates many 4-digit pins, leaving the attacker to guess from a much smaller pool.

The above clock-based random number generator is awful because using the time of day as an *initial seed* is predictable. The initial seed should be much more difficult for an attacker to guess. Good random number generators introduce lots of *entropy* to make their outputs unpredictable. Simply shuffling 4 digits does not introduce much entropy, another reason that our PRNG above would be insecure.

When generating wallets, the user's operating system provides the initial seed / entropy source. Monero then repeatedly applies the Keccak hashing function, to lead to an unpredictable and non-reproducible output. Each round of hashing produces an output that is used as the input for the next hash.

5.3 Generating Monero keys and addresses

5.3.1 Picking a seed

In chapter 2 we talked about the heart of your wallet: its seed. Your wallet generates this secret that is used to derive all of your keys, and access/spend your funds. In that overview, we simply considered the 25-word *seed mnemonic*.

Behind the scenes, a seed is an unique 256-bit integer from which keys and addresses are derived, for example:

112699108505435943726051051450940377552177762677
89095646916738451344467691053980

These are often represented as a 64-digit base-16 number, for example:

```
f9296f587419f1cdede67de160fca14d1069ecaa4c-
52f012af031eeA09ee039c
```

(For mnemonic-style keys, this representation of the seed is actually just the private spend key itself!)

Writing down either of the above key styles would be quite difficult, and most people would be prone to make at least one mistake. Conversion to a seed mnemonic phrase is another step included only for human interpretability and usability. The mnemonic phrase essentially converts the the above 256-bit number into to a *24-digit* (24-word) base-1626 "number" (since there are 1626 words in the seed dictionary). This representation of the long seed strings is much easier to read:

```
lamb hexagon aces acquire twang bluntly argue when
unafraid awning academy nail threaten sailor palace
selfish cadets click sickness juggled border thumbs
remedy ridges border
```

When your wallet presents the 24-word seed, it adds a 25th word that functions as a *checksum*, which allows later detection of typos or mistakes. Monero's mnemonic method encodes with a minimum 4:3 ratio. In other words, four bytes creates three words, plus one checksum word; eight bytes creates six words, plus one checksum word; and so on.

The private view key is derived by hashing the seed with Keccak-256, producing a second 256-bit integer, which is then sent to the function called *sc_reduce32* to ensure that it is compatible with the elliptic curve. The seeds created by this method will always be

116

valid scalars as they are sent to *sc_reduce32* first.

5.3.2 Key derivation

5.3.2.1 All keys

The Monero *seed* described above is actually your *secret spend key*, from which all other keys are derived. The *secret view key* is the reduced hash of your secret spend key, converted to a valid scalar for the ed25519 curve.

These two private keys are multiplied by the generator point to yield the two public keys for your wallet (*public spend* and *public view*). This method for derivating keys is referred to as the *deterministic* method.

5.3.2.2 View-only wallets

You can grant *view-only* access to a Monero account by setting up a wallet with your secret view key, but NOT the secret spend key. These view-only wallets can see all incoming transactions, but cannot spend moneroj or see outgoing transactions.

There are several situations in which it is useful to check incoming transactions without send access. For instance, individuals with cold wallets can use the view key to check that funds arrived, while keeping their secret spend key safely sequestered away. Likewise, developers can build systems that can detect and respond to incoming payments, without needing to have the ability to move those funds.

This feature is especially valuable for charities, which can share their view key to ensure transparency and accountability around donations. If you make a donation to the a public address, you can use the view key to verify that the charity received your funds.

For example, consider the the main Monero donation address: 44AFFq5kSiGBoZ4NMDwYtN18obc8AemS33DBLWs3H7otXft3XjrpDt QGv7SqSsaBYBb98uNbr2VBBEt7f2wfn3RVGQBEP3A.

Since stealth addresses prevent that public address from being recorded or searchable on the blockchain, the community also publishes the view key (f359631075708155cc3d92a32b75a7d02a5d-cf27756707b47a2b31b21c389501) so that the public can review donation activity.

Since anybody with the view key can see the total amount that a wallet has received, a transparent charity that has been gifted 100 XMR cannot divert 90 XMR and claim that they only received 10 XMR. This functionality is especially valuable for crowdfunding situations where a certain donation threshold must be reached.

The inability to see outgoing transactions from a view-only wallet is a feature, not a bug! If the outgoing transactions were made public, it would reveal when an output has been spent. This would be very problematic, since ring signatures rely on spend state ambiguity. Suppose a charity reveals when an output is spent; all appearances in future (and previous) ring signatures can be identified as decoys. Not exposing outgoing transactions is thus necessary for maintaining the integrity of overall network privacy.

5.3.3 Address generation

A Monero wallet's standard address is composed of the two public keys (the public spend key + public view key) derived in the last section. It also contains a checksum and a *network byte* which identifies both the network and the address type.

5.3.3.1 Network byte

The network byte is used differentiating between various crypto-currencies and networks. CryptoNote coins specify the appropriate values in the file `src/CryptoNote_config.h`, for example

```
uint64_t const CRYPTONOTE_PUBLIC_ADDRESS_BASE58_
PREFIX = 18;
```

Monero's main network uses '18' to indicate a primary address (this is why Monero primary addresses begin with a '4,' which is the ASCII representation).

Monero developers use the testnet and stagenet, which have their own unique network bytes:

Name	Code value	ASCII value for prefix
Main net primary address	18	4
Main net subaddress	42	8
Test net primary address	53	9
Test net subaddress	63	B
Stage net primary address	26	5
Stage net subaddress	36	7

5.3.3.2 Concatenated public keys

The public spend key and public view key are concatenated and appended to the network byte, to produce the raw address (everything except the checksum). While this address is still in a raw format, it contains all of the key information: keys for crafting transactions and network metadata to ensure that transactions are announced to the correct network.

5.3.3.3 Checksum

Since Monero transactions are non-reversible, it's crucial to send payments to the right address! To help avoid typos and minor mistakes, the address includes a checksum. If the sender makes a typo or doesn't capture the whole address, the checksum will not match, indicating that the string entered is not a valid address.

This checksum is generated by Keccak hashing the address information collected in the previous section. The hash digest is shortened to the first 4 bytes, and used as the checksum.

5.3.3.4 Bring it all together: address finalization

Lastly, the network byte, keys, and checksum are concatenated according to Monero specification:

Index	Sizes in bytes	Description
0	1	identifies the network and address type - '18' for mainnet and '53' for the testnet (in base-58, '4' and '9' respectively)
1	32	public spend key
33	32	public view key
64	4	checksum (hash created with Keccak function of the previous 65 bytes, trimmed to first 4 bytes)

Lastly, this 69-byte output string is encoded into the Monero base-58 format. This conversion increases the length to a 95-character string that is easy to read and write. That's all there is to it! Monero primary addresses simply contain:

[network byte + public spend key + public view key + checksum]
Example standard address:
```
4BKjy1uVRTPiz4pHyaXXawb82XpzLiowSDd8rEQJGqvN6AD6kWos
LQ6VJXW9sghopxXgQSh1RTd54JdvvCRsXiF41xvfeW5
```

The pseudo-code below describes the process of generating a public address, using Hs() to represent Keccak hashing and '||' to represent string concatenation.

```
    Checksum = Hs(Varint(Prefix) || public spend key ||
public view key)
    SerializedString = Base58(Prefix || public spend key
|| public view key || checksum)
```

Chapter 7 includes actual Python code for generating keys and addresses yourself!

5.3.4 Subaddresses

Privacy for Monero transactions is achieved by three primary constructions: ring signatures, stealth (one-time) addresses, and RingCT. These mitigate the risk of transactions being linked by analyzing blockchain data. However, one must consider risks of "off-chain" linkability (in other words, information collected from other sources besides the blockchain data itself).

For example, suppose your primary address has received payments from several different individuals. Thanks to Monero's stealth address technology, your public address is never explicitly recorded in transactions, so nobody can to link those transactions from analyzing the blockchain (including the spenders). However, this cryptographic privacy is entirely circumvented if two of your senders communicate with each other and discover that they have both been sending moneroj to the same address!

You can avoid this risk by generating multiple subaddresses, sharing a unique one with each sender. The subaddresses are derived from the same keys as your primary address, so funds received to any subaddress will route to the same overall wallet balance. However the various subaddresses are cryptographically unlinkable, so multiple people sending moneroj to the same wallet cannot recognize this by comparing their address lists.

5.3.4.1 Creating a subaddress

Recall that each wallet has two pairs of keys. The private view key (pV_0) and private spend key (pS_0) are kept secret, while the public view key (PV_0) and private spend key (PS_0) are encoded into each address. As discussed, the public keys are generated by multiplying the private keys by the generator point (G) on the elliptic curve, i.e. $(PV_0, PS_0) = (pV_0, pS_0)G$.

Your wallet can create a vast number of subaddresses, each with a different index 'i' (typically starting at $i=1$). Each subaddress will have its own sets of keys at each index, with unique private (pV_1, pS_i) and public (PV_i, PS_i) keys.

The formula to create a public spend key for the ith subaddress is:

$$PS_i = Hs(pV_0 || i)G + PS_0$$

This process begins by concatenating the index 'i' to the primary address private view key (pV_0), and passing that result through the hash_to_scalar function (note: in practice, the reference client wallet also concatenates the string SubAddr to the data, as a common salt for the hashing). The resulting scalar is multiplied by the curve generator point and added to the the primary public spend key through elliptic curve point addition.

This subaddress public spend key is multiplied by the primary private spend key to yield the subaddress public view key:

$$PV_i = pV_0 * PS_i$$

The subaddress public keys are encoded into the public address following the same convention as primary addresses:

```
Subaddress_i = base58(network byte || PS_i || PV_i
|| checksum)
```

However, the mainnet network byte for subaddresses is 0x42, which is why they all begin with the digit an '8'.

5.3.4.2 Sending to a subaddress

This different identifying first network bit is crucial, since transactions to subaddresses must be constructed slightly differently than normal.

When constructing a transaction, wallets typically generate 32 random bytes to serve as the *private key*. When sending to a primary address, this random key is multiplied by the elliptic curve generator point through elliptic curve scalar multiplication to yield the transaction public key. However, when sending to a subaddress, the private transaction key is instead multiplied by the public spend key of the receiving subaddress.

5.3.4.3 Receiving to a subaddress

Due to the obfuscated nature of the Monero blockchain, a wallet must scan every transaction to ascertain whether it belongs to the owner.

To ascertain whether a given output X (with public transaction key R) was sent to the primary address, the wallet checks calculations based on its the public view key and public spend key. If the equality $X==Hs(pV_0*R)G+PS_0$ is true, then that output can be unlocked and spent!

However, the process is slightly different to check which outputs belong to subaddresses. The calculation is mostly the same, except that the hash_to_scalar term is subtracted from the output and compared against subaddress public spend keys. The wallet knows it has found on output that it owns, if the equality $PS_i == X - Hs(pV_0*R)G$ is true.

5.3.5 Other methods for key derivation

To add to the confusion, there are presently at least 3 different methods of private key derivation used in Monero (this is also the case for Bitcoin). These methods vary in a few "key" ways:

- **Original (non-deterministic style):** The private spend key and private view key are both independently and randomly chosen to form an account. There is no good way to backup a non-deterministic account, other than retaining copies of each file. Due to better alternatives, this unwieldy method is no longer recommended.

- **Mnemonic (deterministic or "Electrum") style:** In this style, all of the keys are derived from a single private spend key, which is referred to as the *seed*. The private view key is derived by hashing the private spend key with Keccack-256 to produce a valid EdDSA scalar. These accounts are easy to backup, since you only need to write down the seed (which is usually expressed as a base-1626 *mnemonic phrase*).

- **MyMonero Style:** The MyMonero wallet family uses a method similar to the Electrum convention, however the seed phrase is 13 words instead of the usual 25 words. The 13 words convert to a 128-bit integer that is used for both spend and view key derivation. The seed integer is hashed with Keccak-256 and converted to the private spend key. This private spend key is hashed again with Keccak-256 and converted to the private view key.

You may have noticed a critical difference between the MyMonero and Electrum seed styles. MyMonero creates the private view key by hashing a random integer, whereas the Electrum style hashes the private spend key. This means that the 13 and 25 word seeds are not compatible - it is not possible to create an Electrum-style account that matches a MyMonero-style account (or vice versa) because the view keypair will always be different.

5.4 The privacy technologies

5.4.1 Stealth address

Chapter 3 conceptually described how one-time addresses, also known as stealth addresses, allow transactions to be posted to the network without revealing the recipient's true address. This section will go deeper to explain the cryptography behind that one-time public key.

5.4.1.1 Sending

The CryptoNote protocol calculates the receiving one-time address according to the formula $X = Hs(r*PV|i)G + PS$. Let's step through the meaning of these symbols, and how Maria would generate a one-time address when she sends money to George.

The variable r is the transaction private key, which is a 256-bit pseudorandom scalar. Maria (the sender) is the only person that will ever know this key; even George (the recipient) never learns the random number that Maria's wallet chose for r.

Maria then multiplies George's public view key, PV, by r and then appends the output index, i. This quantity ($r*PV|i$) is then run through the hash_to_scalar function, $Hs()$. This function hashes its inputs using the Keccak-256 algorithm, then takes that resulting hash modulo the prime number
$2^{255} + 2774231777737235353585193779088364 8493$.

The $Hs(r*PV|i)$ term calculated in the above paragraph is multiplied by The ed25519 basepoint, G. Lastly, Maria adds this quantity to George's public spend key, PS, to produce the final output, X, which is the stealth address.

This convoluted process allows Maria to hide the transaction to George on the blockchain, using a randomly-generated one-time address that nobody will be able to connect to him.

5.4.1.2 Receiving

Given how well Maria hid the moneroj that she was sending to George (obscured by a transaction private key that even George doesn't know), you might wonder how he can find it on the blockchain!

As described in chapter 3, George must scan the blockchain for outputs that belong to him. The process is very similar to the method that Maria used to generate the address.

George takes the public transaction key R from the blockchain, and multiplies it by his private view key, pV. Following similar steps as Maria, George appends the output index i and then applies the `hash_to_scalar` function to (pV*R|i). He then multiplies the result by G and adds his own public spend key, PS. If this value matches the output, then it belongs to him.

In other words, George's wallet scans over every transaction in the blockchain to identify outputs for which X = Hs(pV*R|i)G + PS.

5.4.2 Ring Confidential Transactions

Ring Confidential Transactions (RingCT) obscure the amount of moneroj being sent in a transaction. RingCT was implemented in January 2017 and became mandatory in all transactions after September 2017.

Only transactions that mint new moneroj as coinbase rewards have visible amounts, not masked by RingCT. This is an auditing feature that allows any any network participant count and verify exactly how many moneroj have been generated. After this public coin emission, these transactions are converted to RingCT outputs before further use.

All non-coinbase transactions employ RingCT to encrypt the transaction amount. The amount for each transaction is encrypted two different ways, which are both included in the message.

First, the amount is encrypted by a key derived from the public information in the recipient's address. This version is recorded in the ecdhInfo field, and can only be decrypted and read by the recipient, using the transaction shared secret.

Secondly, the amount is integrated into a Pedersen commitment, which allows other Monero users to verify the validity of the transaction themselves. Nobody can retrieve the transaction amount from the Pedersen commitment, however anybody can inspect the result to mathematically verify that the outputs balance the inputs. This prevents any transactions attempting to forge moneroj.

There are two key aspects to RingCT verification:

1. The sender verifiably proves that all outputs contain a positive amount, using a range proof. The range proof demonstrates that the masked number can be generated as the sum of positive powers of 2, without revealing what those powers are. Without range proofs, a sneaky user with 5 XMR could create

a transaction with a pair of outputs containing +13 XMR and -8 XMR.

2. The sender also demonstrates that the inputs balance the outputs, which is non-trivial given that ring signatures contain decoys to prevent the verifying party from knowing the true source of the input funds! Homomorphic Pederson commitments enable the sender to prove that one of the potential inputs has a zero difference with the outputs, without revealing the amount in the process.

For a simple analogy, consider the following example equations. Like masked transaction amounts, you can verify that whether each equation is valid without knowing the value of A.

A = our output, nobody knows that

$5A + 1A + 4A = 10A$ TRUE! Verified, without knowing A

$6A + 4A + 2A = 14A$ FALSE! Not verified, rejected!

5.4.3 Ring signatures

Monero utilizes ring signature technology to protect the privacy of each transaction's sender. A *ring signature* is a type of cryptographic signature that allows one active participant to sign a message on behalf of a group. The private key owned by the active signer is mixed with public key information from the other members to produce a single signature. Anybody can validate the signed message against the public keys to verify that one of the ring members initiated the signature, however it is impossible to ascertain which member contributed the private key.

In the context of Monero, the message is a transaction, authorized by the ring signature. The output that is actually being spent is the true signer, and he public keys from other outputs (from past transactions) are mixed in as *decoy* signers. The actual signer and decoy signers are mathematically equally valid; the resulting ring signature cannot be cryptographically examined to determine which member actively initiated the signature. Consequently, no outside party (including the recipient) can ascertain which of the outputs referenced in a transaction was actually spent.

Every ring signature produces a single key image that is derived from the output actually being spent. This is a cryptographically-secure process: each output corresponds to a single key image, and producing the *key image* does not reveal the true signer in the ring.

When the owner of an output spends it in a new transaction, the network stores the key image that was produced by the ring signature. Since the network cannot identify which outputs are spent, it instead keeps track of which key images are spent! If the owner tried to fraudulently spend the output again, the same key image would be produced, so the network knows to reject the transaction.

Let's dig into the actual mathematics of generating a ring signature. Throughout this example, let H_s be a hash function that returns scalars (in the appropriate field) and H_p be a hash function that returns points (in the appropriate curve group). We purposely avoid formally defining these domains and codomains to avoid complication. Let G be a fixed point known to all parties.

You are going to sign the transaction message M with a ring signature. Monero currently requires eleven ring members for each signature, however let's consider a simplified example with three ring members. You have the keypair (public and private) for the output that you are spending, and select two other outputs (and their public keys) to serve as decoys. Naturally the indexing of the ring members should be randomized, since the cryptographic anonymity would be circumvented if the true signer was always in slot #1. For the simplified example with three ring members, suppose your wallet has randomly selected to put the true source of the funds in slot #2.

You retrieve the public output keys for the decoys (P_1 and P_3) from the blockchain, and you have both the private key (p_2) and the public key ($P_2 = p_2G$) for the output that you are spending. You start by choosing a random number u, which you will later discard. First you form the following commitment, starting at the index after the one you picked for your key:

$$c_3 = H_s(M, uG, uH_p(P_2))$$

To form the rest of the commitments, you also choose random numbers s_3 and s_1 that you'll need later:

$$c_1 = H_s(M, s_3G + c_3P_3, s_3H_p(P_3) + c_3p_2H_p(p_2))$$

Notice that you are including several pieces of information here: the public key P_3 you plucked from the blockchain, the random number s_3 you came up with, the previous commitment c_3, and a value $p_2 H_p(P_2)$ formed from your own key. You keep going:

$$c_2 = H_s(M, s_1G + c_1P_1, s_1H_p(P_1) + c_1p_2H_p(P_2))$$

But you are not quite done! To hide where your actual key is, you cleverly define $s_2 = u - c_2 p_2$. The signature you send to the blockchain and the world contains several quantities: (c_1, s_1, s_2, s_2, J), where $J = p_2 H_p(P_2)$ is the key image used in each commitment. We rename it here to highlight the fact that the public doesn't know the pieces that were used to form it.

Here's why this is clever: by setting $s_2 = u - c_2 p_2$, you can re-arrange to see that $u = s_2 + c_2 p_2$. This means that the public sees the first commitment c_3 that you made as the following:

$$c_3 = H_s(M, s_2 G + c_2 P_2, s_2 H_p(P_2) + c_2 p_2 H_p(P_2))$$

This looks exactly like the other commitments! Although you never broadcast u, you use it to cleverly make each commitment look identical in the eyes of observers. This is the power of the ring signature. Nobody can ascertain which commitment hides your true key, but everybody can mathematically verify for themselves that:

1. the sender knew one of the private keys represented by the public keys
2. the key image was computed correctly

Observe that the key image $J = p_2 H_p(P_2)$ was uniquely calculated from the true output's keypair, without any random numbers or decoys' public keys. Thus, any fraudulent attempts to spend the output a second time will generate an identical key image. Since the network keeps track of which key images have been used, any attempts to reuse outputs are easily detected and rejected.

Note that the above example of a Back-style LSAG ring signature is included for educational purposes, and should not be used as a reference document for production implementations.

5.4.4 Further resources

If you want to venture even further into the calculations behind these technologies, check out Zero to Monero, a highly-technical mathematical tour that is also available as a free community-funded PDF.

5.5 The Monero blockchain

By now you're familiar with the importance and utility of blockchains as distributed public ledgers. These blocks are structured and ordered into an immutable append-only database, secured by cryptographic tools that prevent any tampering or cheating. Monero's blockchain is unique and we'll discuss its technology and specifications in this section.

5.5.1 Lightning Memory Mapped Database

Monero uses the Lightning Memory Mapped Database (LMDB) system to store its blockchain. LMDB is a software library that provides a high-performance embedded transactional database in the form of a key-value store. This means that it is highly effective, and easy to search.

LMDB is written in C++ with API bindings several programming languages, and is developed by Symas Corporation. Here are a few LMDB features:

- Arbitrary key/data pairs storage as byte arrays
- Range-based search capability
- Support for a single key with multiple data items
- Advanced methods for appending records at the end of the

database, which gives a dramatic write performance increase over other similar stores

5.5.2 The structure of a block

The CryptoNote standards define specifications for storing and delineating data within blocks and on the blockchain. The block structure contains three main components:

- The block header
- The *base transaction*
- A list of transaction identifiers (hashes of transactions mined in the block)

5.5.2.1 The block header

Each block starts with a header that contains key metadata. The "major_version" defines the block header parsing rules, so it can be interpreted correctly. The "minor_version" defines the interpretation details that are not related to the main header parsing.

Even if the minor version is unknown, it is always safe to parse the block header of a particular major version. Parsing the block header with an unknown major version is risky, since the contents of the block header may be misinterpreted.

Field	Type	Content
major_version	varint	Major block header version
minor_version	varint	Minor block header version

»

timestamp	varint	Block creation time (UNIX timestamp)
prev_id	hash	Identifier of the previous block
nonce	4 bytes	Any value which is used in the network consensus algorithm

5.5.2.2 Base Transaction

Each valid block contains a single *base transaction* that routes its coinbase reward to the miner. The base transaction must follow the coin emission rules, and include the block height field.

5.5.2.3 List of transaction identifiers

Field	Type	Content
version	varint	Transaction format version
unlock_time	varint	UNIX timestamp.
input_num	varint	Number of inputs. Always 1 for base transactions.
input_type	byte	Always 0xff for base transactions
height	varint	Height of the block which contains the transaction
output_num	varint	Number of outputs
outputs	array	Lists of outputs as array

The base transaction is followed by a list of transaction identifiers. These identifiers are calculated by taking the Keccak hash of the transaction body. The list starts with the number of identifiers and is followed by the identifiers themselves (if the block is not empty).

5.5.2.4 Calculation of Block Identifier

The identifier of a block is produced by hashing the following data with Keccak-256:

- size of block_header
- block_header
- Merkle root hash
- number of transactions (varint)

The Merkle root hash "attaches" the transactions referenced in the block's body to the block header: once the Merkle root hash is fixed, the transactions cannot be modified. This security feature keeps blockchains safe from tampering or any kind of retroactive modification.

5.5.3 The mining economy

Block rewards and fees were mentioned conceptually in chapters 2 and 4. Now you'll actually learn about the complexities of block sizes, rewards, and the relationship with fees.

5.5.3.1 Mining coinbase reward

As discussed in Chapter 4, all moneroj originate as rewards paid to miners for successfully completing blocks. The size of this coinbase payment depends on the the current supply (A) and the initial number of atomic units (S = 2^{64} - 1). An atomic unit is the smallest division of Monero currently recognized by the network (1×10^{-12} XMR)

```
Base Reward = 2 * ((S - A) * 2⁻²⁰ * 10⁻¹²)
```

Monero has a *tail emission*, which is a small fixed base reward that will continue after most of the supply has been mined. Monero's minimum base reward is 0.6 XMR per block, so miners will never have to subsist on fees alone.

5.5.3.2 Dynamic block size

Monero has a dynamic block size, which allows for continuous adjustment as the network grows, in contrast to many cryptocurrencies that use a static (fixed) block size. For example, Bitcoin's initial 1 MB fixed block size caused scaling issues, by limiting the number of transactions that could be included in each block (consequently limiting the overall transaction volume for the network). In 2017, this bottleneck resulted in periods with extremely high fees and delayed processing of transactions. Various proposed solutions were put forth, resulting in a period of contentious debate.

To avoid these issues, Monero uses a dynamic block size mechanism that allows the miners to use a larger blocks to accommodate increased traffic. However, if the block size was left entirely unconstrained, the Monero network could be vulnerable to spam attacks, i.e. lots of small transactions designed to exhaust network and storage resources by making the blockchain expand too rapidly.

To prevent excessive blocksize growth, Monero mining protocols includes a *penalty function* that decreases the coinbase reward for oversize blocks. The original CryptoNote authors included this consensus rule to limit the rate of block size expansion and avoid rapid blockchain bloat.

If a block is mined with size (B) that is is larger the median size of the last 100 blocks (M_N), part of the base reward is withheld, according to:

```
Penalty = BaseReward * ((B / M ) - 1)²
                               N
```

Miners receive the full reward for any sized block up to 300 kB; for anything larger, the penalty function "kicks in". The maximum block size is $2*M_N$, at which point the entire coinbase is withheld.

5.5.3.3 Fees

When transaction volume is low and block sizes are small, miners are rewarded with the full coinbase, and fees are minimal.

However, imagine a different scenario: What happens if the median size of the last 100 blocks grows larger than the penalty-free block size (300 kB)? Then, the dynamic fee algorithm comes into play!

Fees are calculated by the weight in of the transaction in kB. Larger ("heavier") transaction incur a higher fee. The dynamic fee calculation is complex, taking into account several factors of the Monero ecosystem, and the transaction's priority (the sender can incentivize miners to quickly include an urgent transaction by attaching a larger fee). The fees necessary to be competitive in an upcoming block are calculated according to:

$$\text{Fee per kB} = (R/R_0) * (M_0/M) * F_0 * (60/300) * 4$$

- R is the base reward
- R_0 is the reference base reward (10 XMR)
- M is the block size limit
- M_0 is the minimum block size limit (300 kB)
- F_0 is 0.002 XMR
- 60/300 is the adjustment factor to account for the increase of the penalty-free block size limit (adjusted from 60 kB to 300 kB in 2017)
- 4 is the adjustment factor to account for the default fee multiplier (the lowest fee level uses a multiplier of x1, and a normal priority transaction uses x4)

Thus, the fees take into account the increase in the median block size relative to the minimum block size. For example, a 600 kB block size (twice the minimum) reduces the fees by half.

Ideally, an increase Monero's exchange rate and usage would result in a reduction of absolute fees (i.e. in terms of XMR). This fee reduction mechanism has less effectiveness during extreme price increases that are disproportionately larger than the increase in transaction volume (and thus block size).

The dynamic fee algorithm is designed to function when the median block size is consistently above 300 kB. While the system is intended to account for increases in price, usage is not perfectly correlated with price, and is thus an imperfect proxy.

5.5.4 Bulletproofs

Bulletproofs are a new feature that dramatically decreases transaction size, which in turn reduces the overall fees per transaction! Monero transactions used to be quite large (usually > 12 kB), so bulletproofs were a much-anticipated enhancement.

Monero's privacy features necessitate several complex "tests" during transaction validation, in order to prevent abuse and spam. This includes verification of masked amounts, checking fees, and confirming that no double spends are occurring.

Most developers have encountered "overflow" errors, when an operation creates a value outside the range that can be represented. Unfortunately, "infinite" is an abstract concept for electronics, which encounter many obstacles with large numbers.

Since RingCT hides the transaction amounts, complicated calculations are necessary to verify that the inputs and outputs balance properly. The useful algebraic properties of commitments are valuable for enabling masked transactions whose validity can be confirmed by any participant.

However, it is also crucial to ensure that each amount is a positive value that will not cause an overflow. This is where range proofs come in, by allowing anybody to verify that a commitment represents an amount within a specified range, without revealing anything else about its value. Each range proof used to require ~ 7 kB, so they made up the bulk of a transaction's size. Most transactions have two outputs (the destination and change address) necessitating at least ~12 kB.

Bulletproofs employ some clever mathematical tricks to construct the range proof with a more efficient mechanism. This reduces the size of a single range proof to ~2 kB!

Before bulletproofs, transactions with multiple outputs required

140

multiple separate range proofs. Consequently, transaction size scaled linearly with the number of outputs (e.g. 1 output = 7 kB, 2 outputs = 14 kB). With bulletproofs, size instead scales logarithmically with more outputs (e.g. 1 output = 2 kB, 2 outputs = 2.5 kB).

By reducing the size of each range proof, and allowing them to combine in a more efficient way, bulletproofs dramatically decrease transaction size, and thus fees. Bulletproofs were enabled by the Monero v0.13.0 network upgrade in October 2018, as an opt-in feature that will become mandatory during the subsequent upgrade.

## Chapter 6

Community and contributing

The Monero Project is a collaborative open community, and we welcome your contributions to code or other facets of the ecosystem. This chapter provides a high-level overview of our decentralized structure, and contains tips and links for getting involved.

6.1 Community culture

6.1.1 Principles of openness

While the Monero cryptocurrency itself epitomizes privacy, its community is built on the core values of transparency and collaboration! Users, developers, and researchers communicate on IRC channels that are open to the public. You can also find an active community of Monero users and developers on other platforms such as Slack, Mattermost, and Taiga. Key meetings are archived for public access on the official website.

This culture of cooperation and openness is a natural consequence of Monero's origin as a code fork from ByteCoin. The developer of ByteCoin operated with unilateral secrecy, making designs and decisions without community feedback. The resulting development mistakes, especially the egregious premine, ruined the viability of the coin.

The Monero community came into existence by forking the shadowy ByteCoin development into the light of a decentralized, collaborative, and diverse community. This has undoubtedly strengthened the project on many fronts, and the Monero community has learned to thrive through cooperation. While cryptography provides the technical underpinnings for Monero, the community is its real source of power!

6.1.2 Many great minds work on Monero

The Monero project is a massive community effort, collectively crafted by hundreds of individuals from all across the globe. At the time of writing, more than 500 people have contributed code, including 200 in the last year. Monero has adopted an *un-governance* scheme for organizing growth and development. The project is comprised of several different *branches* working together: the Monero Core Team, the Monero Research Lab, Monero Workgroups, and the community.

The Monero Core Team manages many of the critical tasks for Monero. Key roles include:

- Acting as primary trusted arbiters of the Forum Funding System on behalf of the community.

- Managing the codebase of the Monero Project, which includes merging code, keeping backups, and ensuring the safety, security, and free access of the code for any party.

- Acting as stewards for the general donation fund, directing its capital toward endeavors that further the Monero Project.

- Acting as trusted signers and distributors of Monero software and related technologies.

- Working with the community to discern a vision and roadmap for leading the Monero Project.

The Monero Research Lab conducts cutting-edge basic and applied research on cryptocurrency technologies and analyses. MRL includes many academics and researchers, and studies are published openly at https://lab.getmonero.org/

The Monero Workgroups are collaborations formed to join people around unique goals. This allows small teams of individuals to connect and tackle specific tasks. For example, the Monero Hardware Workgroup is well underway on its mission to build the first open-source community-driven hardware wallet. Another instance was the Monero Integrations Workgroup, which developed open-source payment gateways. You can join a workgroup to help with translating Monero, crafting kits for Meetups, or helping users with software issues.

Ultimately, it is the incredible **community** that makes Monero possible! Anybody is welcome to contribute code, propose projects, fund proposals, help with outreach, or write books about Monero.

6.2 Code culture

6.2.1 Create a pull request for the improvements

Anyone is welcome to contribute to Monero's codebase! If you have a fix or code change, feel free to submit it as a pull request directly to the "master" branch. To modify the Monero code, follow this process to edit a forked copy and recommend your improvements to the main repository:

1. Fork the repository on GitHub
2. Clone the repository to your machine
3. Make a branch, implement necessary changes
4. Commit the files with a clear descriptive message
5. Execute `git push origin branch-name` to sync the local changes to your forked repository
6. Create a pull request (including clear descriptions and documentation) to submit your changes back to the original (base) repository

Your modifications may be approved quickly if the change is relatively small or does not affect other parts of the codebase. However, changes that are particularly large or complex should be discussed at length with the community.

When submitting a pull request on GitHub, make sure your branch is rebased. Avoid leaving stray and merge commits from other coders in the branch you will submit. You may be asked to rebase if there are conflicts (even if they are trivially-resolvable).

6.2.2 Patch etiquette

Patches should ideally be submitted as pull requests, following the process described above. If that can't be done, patches in `git format-patch` format can be sent (e.g. post to fpaste.org with a long timeout, then share a link with `#monero-dev` on `irc.freenode.net`).

Patches should be self-contained. A good rule of thumb is to create one patch per separate issue, feature, or logical change. Follow the code style of the particular portion of code that you're modifying, and avoid making other unnecessary edits, such as whitespace changes or reindentation. Proper squashing should be done (e.g. if one of your patches includes a bug that is fixed in a subsequent patch, then both patches should be merged).

6.2.3 General guidelines

Commit messages should be sensible. The subject line must describe the patch, with an optional longer body for providing details, documentation, etc. Well-commented code is strongly encouraged, to help others interpret and constructively interact with your code. If your modifications add new functionality, it is helpful to include testing results with your pull request.

If you've made random unrelated changes (including those due to an overzealous editor), you can select which modifications are included in the commit using `git add -p`, which steps through each of the edits to confirm which should be included. This helps create clean patches without any irrelevant changes. `git diff` displays changes in your tree, and `git diff --cached` will show

146

the changes that are currently staged for commit. Hunks that are added with `git add -p`, will "move" from the `git diff` output to the `git diff --cached` output, so you can see clearly what your commit is going to look like.

More specific guidelines regarding common processes are described on the official repository of the Monero Project.

6.2.4 Repository for Monero

Many different repositories are hosted at the Monero Project GitHub. Several of them house components that we've already discussed in *Mastering Monero*, for example:

- Monero: the core of Monero network which includes the Monero Wallet CLI, written in C++ language
- Monero-site: source code for the https://getmonero.org website
- Monero-GUI: Graphical User Interface for Monero, built with Qt library
- kastelo: the community hardware wallet
- kovri: The Kovri anonymizing router

These projects are well-documented, so that you can become familiar with the code and make improvements! There are many sub-projects with a variety of opportunities for you to contribute to Monero. Please visit one of the repositories, read through some of the open issues, and consider how you can leave your legacy in the Monero codebase.

```
$ This text is a terminal command. Don't run this
command if you don't know what you are touching.
```

Note: At the time of writing, some components of the Monero ecosystem are shifting their repositories from GitHub to GitLab.

6.3 Introduction to Monero development

Building the Monero code is a complex process, so some tips and summaries are included here. Linux systems have a built-in shell that helps with building the Monero core, so consider switching to a Unix-based operating system, if possible. Monero is written in C++, with C++11-style referenciation.

6.3.1 Downloading the Monero source code

Monero uses Git for version control; this system allows developers to track changes and modifications to their code, and easily coordinate work on shared files. To download the Monero code, simply execute:

```
$ git clone --recursive https://
github.com/monero-project/monero
```

6.3.2 Dependencies

To build Monero software from the source code, your path will need to include the dependencies in the table below. A few of the libraries are also included in this repository (marked as *Vendored*). By default, the build uses the library installed on the system, and ignores the vendored sources. However, if no library is found installed on the system, then the vendored source will be built and used.

GCC	libunbound	ldns
CMake	libsodium	expat
pkg-config	libminiupnpc	GTest
Boost	libunwind	Doxygen
OpenSSL	liblzma	Graphviz
libzmq	libreadline	pcsclite

6.3.4 Building instruction

Monero uses the CMake build system and a top-level makefile that invokes cmake commands, as needed. Once you've installed the dependences, change to the root of the source code directory and execute the `make` command to begin the build. The process may take up to an hour or two. Once the code has finished building, you can find the Monero binaries in the `build` folder.

6.3.5 Build troubleshooting

If you encounter errors, the output will typically indicate exactly what went wrong. A few of the common bugs to troubleshoot include:

- An outdated boost version (you may have to manually install the current one)
- Outdated gcc/g++
- Missing libzmq3-dev
- Missing libreadline-dev
- OpenGL errors

You can (optionally) type `make debug` to compile a debugging build. There are many communities with information to help you with troubleshooting. Search engine queries with your build errors are likely to connect you with a solution or people that can help.

6.3.6 Building Monero Graphical User Interface

The Monero graphical user interface (GUI) is built with C++ and Qt libraries. Both are necessary to successfully build the GUI. With the dependencies in place, you can clone and build the GUI with the commands:

```
$ git clone --recursive https://github.
com/monero-project/monero-gui
$ cd monero-gui
$ ./build.sh
```

## Chapter 7

Monero integration for developers

T his chapter covers standards and protocols that developers can use to interact with Monero and build new tools. First, the OpenAlias and Monero URI formats are introduced, as effective ways to communicate addresses and other key details. The rest of the chapter discusses remote procedure calls with integration examples in C++ and python.

7.1 OpenAlias: convenient addresses in text (for humans)

It is extremely tricky for anybody without photographic memory to intuitively read and memorize cryptocurrency addresses. A real-life location like "123 Main St" or an email destination like "donate@ masteringmonero.com" is much easier to interpret and recall than a Monero address, such as "45ttEikQEZWN1m7VxaVN9rjQkpSd-mpGZ82GwUps66neQ1PqbQM no4wMY8F5jiDt2GoHzCtMwa7P-DPJUJYb1GYrMP4CwAwNp".

These cryptocurrency addresses contain a lot of information, but are unwieldy for humans. In fact, there is a famous trilemma known as _Zooko's triangle_ that describes the inherent difficulty of designing name systems that simultaneously meet three criteria: secure, decentralized, and human-meaningful.

The Monero address posted above is not remotely "human-meaningful," however it successfully fulfills the other two criteria. Monero public addresses are at least 95 characters long, which is difficult to read and nigh impossible to memorize. Certainly there must be a way to simplify payment destinations!

The Monero Core Team released the OpenAlias standard to "square" Zooko's triangle by creating a human-readable way to communicate addresses. The OpenAlias standard is a text DNS record on a fully-qualified domain name (FQDN). Each text record need only contain two pieces of information: the *prefix*, and the *recipient address*. A `recipient_name` key-value pair can be added as well, however it is not necessary. A typical OpenAlias text record looks like:

```
oa1:xmr
```

```
recipient_address=45ttEikQEZWN1m7VxaVN9rjQkpSd-
mpGZ82Gw Ups66neQ1PqbQMno4wMY8F5jiDt2GoHzCtMwa7P-
DPJUJYb1GYrMP4C wAwNp
```

```
recipient_name=MoneroFFS
```

The "oa1:xmr" portion indicates that the record is based on OpenAlias version 1, and that the destination is a Monero address. A recipient name can be optionally specified, in this case "MoneroFFS".

Name	Size in byte	Description
oa1:	4	The record always starts with "oa1:", which indicates it is an OpenAlias Version 1 record. If we don't have that prefix we ignore the record, as it may be an SPF record or something else that we don't care about.

»

Name	Size in byte	Description
symbol	3	The code for cryptocurrency. The code should follow the ISO 4217 Rules: for example for Monero cryptocurrency the simbol is xmr and for Bitcoin the symbol is btc.
recipient_address = address;	17 + address + 1	The recipient address. The format is recipient_address=your_address; where your_address is your cryptocoin address. For Monero, it will be a 95 characters string. Key-value pairs are separated by a semi-colon and, optionally, a space for legibility. This key-value must exist. OpenAlias exists to alias FQDNs to an "address" of any type, and this is expressed in this value.
recipient_name = description;	14 + description + 1	This is not necessary, but useful for the purpose of confirming the correct recipient with the user, or for providing the user with the option of adding an entry to an address book.

The OpenAlias standard is extensible for developers, intuitive for users, and interoperable between both centralized and decentralized domain systems. The standard can be used with any cryptocurrency, and is already implemented by Monero, Bitcoin (Electrum) and HyperStake.

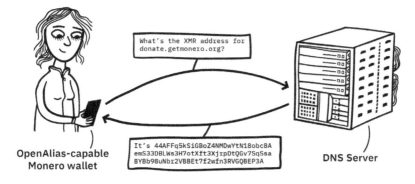

Figure 7.1 - The user-readable donate.getmonero.org is resolved by the DNS server, which sends back the donation address 44AFFq5kSiGBoZ4NMDwYt-N18obc8AemS33DBLWs3H7otXft3XjrpDtQGv7SqSsaBYBb98uNbr2VB-BEt7f2wfn3RVGQBEP3A.

7.2 Monero_URI: convenient info in text (for computers)

The Monero uniform resource identifier standard describes a format for unambiguously communicating key data fields for invoices and transactions. These URIs are especially handy for merchandising purposes such as generating QR codes for payments.

Monero's URI syntax follows RFC 3986, and spaces must be x-www-urlencoded as %20. The example URI below URL shows a an example string that encodes a request for a 0.0413 XMR payment sent to address 4BKq...feW5 for the "Mastering Monero book."

```
monero:4BKjy1uVRTPiz4pHyaXXawb82XpzLiowSDd8rEQJGq-
vN6AD6kWosLQ6VJXW9sghopxXgQSh1RTd54JdvvCRsXiF41x-
vfeW5?tx_amount=0.0413&tx_description=Mastering%20Mone-
ro%20Book
```

Parameter	Type	Description
address	String	The raw address
tx_payment_id	String	The proposed payment ID of the transaction. (if mentioned)
recipient_name	String	The proposed contact name of the recipient. (if mentioned)
tx_amount	Float	The proposed amount of the transaction in atomic currency units.

»

Parameter	Type	Description
tx_description	String	Describes the transaction which should be initiated.

 Use this QR Code to donate 0.05 XMR to the development fund for Monero project.

Check always if the URL is the following:
```
monero:44AFFq5kSiGBoZ4NMDwYtN18obc8AemS33D-
BLWs3H7otXft3XjrpDtQGv7SqSsaBYBb98uNbr2VBBEt-
7f2wfn3RVGQBEP3A?tx_amount=0.05&tx_descrip-
tion=Donation%from%Mastering%20Monero%20Book
```

7.3 Monero RPC

Developers integrating Monero can choose whether to utilize Monero's C++ API (C/C++) or the remote procedure call (RPC) interface. The RPC methods can be accessed by any programming language with the ability to make HTTP requests, so we'll take advantage of this flexibility and include example code for some common tasks.

The Monero daemon (monerod) is accessible via RPC for key activities such as checking balances or sending funds. The Monero wallet RPC (monero-wallet-RPC) allows you to manage all wallet functionality through JSON calls.

The RPC expresses Monero amounts in "atomic units", which refers to the smallest fraction of a Monero coin that is recognized by the current monerod implementation. You can convert easily between formats using:

1 XMR = 1×10^{12} atomic units

7.3.1 Initialization and configuration (setup & secure)

First, launch the Monero wallet RPC, specifying the port and location of your wallet file:

```
$ ./monero-wallet-rpc --rpc-bind-port 18082
--disable-rpc-login --log-level 2 --wallet-file
your-wallet-file --prompt-for-password
```

If you wish to use a remote node, simply add the `--daemon-address` flag followed by its address, for example:

```
--daemon-address node.moneroworld.com:18089
```

Since `monero-wallet-rpc` doesn't bind your IP address and the port by default, you must specify `--rpc-bind-ip yourip` to connect remotely.

A few security precautions are recommended, since rolling into production with an open RPC interface is like going on a safari with no protection! Be sure to set a username and password before your node is exposed. If you follow these steps to put proper safeguards in place, your API will be safe.

The `--restricted-rpc` flag is extremely helpful for limiting RPC privileges to avoid potential abuse. For example, the restricted mode ensures that your node will not return privacy-sensitive data by RPC, and prevents external users from activating mining on your devices.

7.3.2 JSON RPC Format

JSON-RPC is a stateless, lightweight RPC protocol, using the JSON RFC 4672 data format. The specification primarily defines several data structures, and the rules for processing them. The protocol is *transport-agnostic*, meaning that its function is independent of the underlying transport mechanism. Thus, the same concepts can be applied within a given process, over sockets, through HTTP connections, or any other communication channel.

In order to receive any information from the wallet RPC, you must send a message with the **POST** method. The JSON-RPC API accepts messages with the format:

```
{ "jsonrpc" : version , "method" : method,
"params": params, "id": id }
```

using inputs described by:

Field	Description
version	JSON RPC protocol version (Monero supports v2.0)
method	declare which functionality is called
params	specify additional information needed for the desired method
id	number for tracking responses (integers starting from 0)

7.3.3 Example RPC calls

Monero's RPC can be accessed directly from a terminal, as shown in the following examples. The Monero website hosts thorough documentation describing the specifications and full functionality of the wallet RPC and daemon RPC.

7.3.3.1 Get balance

A wallet's balance can be queried by the `getbalance` method:

```
$ curl -X POST 127.0.0.1:18082/json_rpc -d
'{"jsonrpc":"2.0","id":"0","method":"getbal-
ance"}' -H 'Content-Type: application/json'
```

which returns two outputs: the [total] `balance` and the `unlocked_balance`, which only includes transactions deep enough in the blockchain to be considered "safe" for spending (e.g. confirmed as available after 6 blocks).

```
{"id": "0","jsonrpc": "2.0", "re-
sult": {  "balance": 140000000000, "un-
locked_balance": 84000000000} }
```

In this case, the wallet contains 0.14 XMR, and only 0.084 XMR unlocked.

7.3.3.2 Get address

Query the wallet's address.

```
$ curl -X POST 127.0.0.1:18082/json_rpc -d
'{"jsonrpc":"2.0","id":"0","method":"getad-
dress"}' -H 'Content-Type: application/json'
```

which returns :

```
{"id": 0,"jsonrpc": "2.0","result": {"ad-
dress": "42uMGYwvLuUGJzqdWZvr47CGCBz1qNNEx-
ZeegcjLPMbaFkBb3XG g6Y1bUwaMbovzGWDXtaASxS-
BYtaiBB4wuDmrAMCygexH", "addresses": [{
"address":   "42uMGYwvLuUGJzqdWZvr47CGCBz1qN-
NExZeegcjLPMbaFkBb3XG g6Y1bUwaMbovzGWDXtaASx-
SBYtaiBB4wuDmrAMCygexH", "address_index": 0,
"label": "Primary account","used": false
          },
          {
                "address": "894PaGJyxRjZU8nP-
7Dh4FuAyzr2dK3VT9ZZX95MxdAGP3HoHEpA bNb8Htg-
p5LKzc1pXQ8zhpokTZtcUTnzeU823oUPUGSpv",
                "address_index": 1,
                "label": "",
                "used": false
          },
                              ]
    }
}
```

7.3.3.3 Create address

Create a new address for an account. Optionally, label the new
address.

```
$ curl -X POST 127.0.0.1:18082/json_rpc -d '{"json-
rpc":"2.0","id":"0","method":"create_address",
"params" : "{"account_index:0,"label":"Secondary
account"}}' -H 'Content-Type: application/json'
{
    "id": 0, "jsonrpc": "2.0", "result": {
    "address": "86KoCQsZHQvSUnp9fFn-
92e5QGUiZtH1qZ1nNx1Jv5eJs94ywbLR2k 11CjZ-
Tq5o4v8j9bx3CEAturCheJqJR7cYdQKT4xE3w",
"address_index": 9
    }
}
```

7.3.3.4 Create account

Create an account

```
$ curl -X POST 127.0.0.1:18082/json_rpc -d
'{"jsonrpc":"2.0","id":"0","method":"cre-
ate_account", "params":{"label":"Secondary ac-
count"}}' -H 'Content-Type: application/json'
```

```
{
  "id": "0",
  "jsonrpc": "2.0",
  "result": {
    "account_index": 1,
    "address": "88bV1uo76AaKZaWD389kCf5Ef-
PxKFYEKUQbs9ZRJm23E2X2oYgV9b Q54FiY-
6hAB83aDXMUSZF6KWyfeQqzLqaAeeFrk9iic"
  }
}
```

7.3.3.5 Transfer

Transfer (send) an amount of Monero, specified in atomic units.

```
$ curl -X POST http://127.0.0.1:18082/json_rpc -d
' {"jsonrpc":"2.0", "id":"0", "method":"transfer",
"params":{"destinations": [{"amount":100000000,
 "address":"9wNgSYy2F9qPZu7KBjvsFgZLTKE2TZgE-
pNFbGka9gA5 zPmAXS35QzzYaLKJRkYTnzgArGNX7T-
vSqZC87tBLwtaC5RQgJ8rm" }, {"amount":200000000,
 "address":"9vH5D7Fv47mbpCpdcthcjU34rqiiAYRCh1tYy-
wmhqnE k9iwCE9yppgNCXAyVHG5qJt2kExa42TuhzQfJbmb-
peGLkVbg8xit" }],"mixin":4,"get_tx_key":
true}}' -H 'Content-Type: application/json'
{
  "id": "0",
  "jsonrpc": "2.0",
  "result": {
    "fee": 48958481211,
"tx_hash": "985180f468637bc6d-
2f72ee054e1e34b8d5097988bb29a2e0cb 763e4464db23c",
    "tx_key": "8d62e5637f1fcc9a8904057d6bed-
6c697618507b193e956f77c 31ce662b2ee07",
    "amount": 300000000,
    "tx_blob": "",
    "tx_metadata": "",
    "multisig_txset": ""
  }
}
```

7.4 Monero integration in practice (Python and C++ tutorials)

Picking the coding language for these examples is tricky, since every developer knows that there's no perfect universal programming language. However, Python is well-suited for Mastering Monero, since it is a free and open-source scripting language that is relatively approachable and comprehensible for novices.

The following examples use the newest version, Python 3. Most Debian-based Linux distributions ship with Python 2 and Python 3 pre-installed. Before starting, you should update and upgrade your software to ensure that necessary resources are up-to-date:

```
$ sudo apt-get update && sudo apt-get -y upgrade
```

The code for the following tutorials is freely available on a public repository. You can directly download the exercises through the powerful 'git' control version system using the command:

Each tutorial is located on a folder. For example, "Tutorial 1" will be tutorial-1. To download the resources via Git versioning system, simply execute:

```
$ git clone https://github.com/monerobook/code
```

7.4.1 Tutorial 1 - Get your balance

This program will connect to the daemon via RPC, then query and print the account balance. From the section introducing RPC, you might remember the `getbalance` function (also responds to `get_balance`).

We'll start by importing two Python libraries that are very useful for making POST requests in python: 'requests' and 'json'.

```
# Mastering Monero Tutorial. This is a comment
import requests
import json
```

Let's preemptively store some of the information in variables to avoid cluttering up the requests:

```
## Import Setup variables
## Url for JSON RPC interface. We assume that your RPC
interface is running on localhost port 18082
url = "http://localhost:18082/json_rpc"

## JSON headers . Required
headers = {'content-type': 'application/json'}

## RPC input . Adding method name , at the moment we don't
need variables.

rpc_fields = {
        "method" : "get_balance"
}
```

Recall the standard JSON fields that should be included in an RPC call:

```
# Adding the JSON RPC version and id. Id is a int variable
which should be incremented each request. First request
is 0 , second is one and ...
rpc_fields.update({"jsonrpc": "2.0", "id": "0"})
```

Now everything is prepared, so there's only one thing left to do! Send all the variables to the JSON RPC interface using the POST HTTP method:

```
# execute the rpc request
response = requests.post(url,data=json.dumps(rpc_input),-
headers=headers)
# print the response as JSON
print(json.dumps(response.json()))
```

Save all the above code as tutorial.py (or any name of your choice) and execute:

```
$ python tutorial.py
```

Your script should print the output of the getbalances call into your terminal:

```
{
    "id": "0",
    "jsonrpc": "2.0",
    "result": {
        "balance": 0,
        "multisig_import_needed": false,
        "unlocked_balance": 0 }
}
```

While this contains all of the information we need, the output RPC syntax is not formatted for optimal human readability. Staring at too many {}'s can become disorienting after a while!

For a cleaner output, we can add a few lines of code to the bottom of the tutorial script, so that it only prints the balance (or unlocked balance, if you'd prefer).

```python
# Get the balance from response array and convert to a
string.
balance = str(response.json().get('result').get('balance'))

print("Balance is " + balance )
```

Now, running

```
$ python tutorial.py
```

Should simply return:

```
Balance is 426700000
```

You can use RPC methods like this to develop your own personal client for your Monero wallet!

7.4.2 Tutorial 2 - How to generate a pseudo-random address

In chapter 5, we introduced the concept of pseudo-random address generation. To augment the mathematical explanation, here is a python implementation for you to follow.

First, import necessary libraries and add them to the path.

```
# Import libraries. Hexlify for hex code, utils for the
utility, etc.
import os, sys
from binascii import hexlify, unhexlify
sys.path.append('../libraries')
import utils
import ed25519
import base58
```

To code the function `generate_random_address`, several steps must be included:

1) Create your seed by pseudo-randomly generating a 32 byte (256-bit) random number. Use the hexlify library to convert your seed to a hex-encoded string, stored in the variable `seed`.

2) Record your secret spend key by reducing the seed to a valid scalar for the ed25519 elliptic curve. Your secret spend key is simply this representation of your seed. Verification requires the `sc_reduce32` function from the `utils` library.

3) Calculate your secret view key as the reduced hash of your secret spend key. The `hash_to_scalar` function hashes the input, then converts it to a valid scalar for the ed25519 elliptic curve.

4) <u>Derive public keys</u> by using the `publickey_to_private_key` function to multiply your private keys by the generator point. Your secret spend key yields your public spend key, and likewise your secret view key is used to derive your public view key.

5) <u>Begin building your public address</u> by concatenating the network byte (0x12 for public Monero addresses), the public spend key, and the public view key. These are the key pieces of information included in every Monero address.

6) <u>Calculate the checksum</u> that will be appended to the above string by taking the first 4 bytes (8 hex characters) of its Keccak-256 hash.

7) <u>Encode the info + checksum</u> in Base 58 representation for human-readability. That's all there is to it! As discussed in Chapter 5, Monero addresses consist of:

[network byte + public spend key + public view key + checksum]

```
def generate_random_address():
    ## Generate 32 bytes (256 bits) of pseudo-random data
    seed = hexlify(os.urandom(32))

    ## Reduce random data to make it a valid ed25519 scalar
    secret_spend_key = utils.sc_reduce32(seed)

    ## Use a reduced hash of the secret spend key for the
deterministic secret view key
    secret_view_key = utils.hash_to_scalar(secret_spend_key)
```

Continues on next page »

```
    ## multiply by the generator point to get public keys
from private keys
    public_spend_key = utils.publickey_to_privatekey(se-
cret_spend_key)
    public_view_key  = utils.publickey_to_privatekey(se-
cret_ view_key)
    ## the network byte, public spend key, and public view
key are all concatenated together
    ## 0x12 is the Monero mainnet network byte
    network_byte = "12"
    ## Concatenate the three strings
   data = network_byte + public_spend_key + public_view_key
   hash = utils.keccak_256(data)
    ## checksum is the first 4 bytes (8 hex characters) of
the hash of the previous data
    checksum = hash[0:8]
    address = base58.encode(data + checksum)

    ## Printing the keys

    print("Secret_spend_key : " + secret_spend_key)
    print("Secret_view_key : " + secret_view_key)
    print("Public_spend_key : " + public_spend_key)
    print("Public_view_key : " + public_view_key)

    ## Returning address generated
    return address
```

End

7.4.3 Tutorial 3 - Vanity address generator

Vanity addresses refer to cryptocurrency addresses generated to have some particular prefix that you choose. If you want an address with a "cat" name, you can use this method to generate a public address beginning with "4cat". There are some limitations due to the Monero address format: You cannot remove the initial 4 (the hex-encoded network byte, 0x12) and the base 58 encoding excludes some characters (I,l,0,O).

You should never trust website or third party that generates vanity cryptocurrency addresses for you. There is no way to know whether those keys were generated securely and not retained by the service or a snoop.

Here is a small Python script that you can code and verify yourself, to safely generate your own vanity addresses. The approach is simple: repeatedly generate addresses until one of the results matches your criteria. Short vanity strings are recommended, since the time necessary to brute force a qualifying address increases dramatically as the length of the target string increases.

Most of the code is contained in `while(1)`, an infinite loop that will run until a matching address is discovered. With each iteration through the loop, it calls the `generate_random_address` function from the previous example for a fresh address.

As soon as the address is created, the script checks whether the first characters match the user's desired input. When a suitable address is discovered, then the script prints the address and exits, breaking the while loop.

```
import sys
sys.path.append('../libraries')
import address

if (len(sys.argv) != 2):
    print("usage: python vanity_address.py [desired_prefix]")
    exit()

if (sys.argv[1][0] != "4"):
    print "Monero addresses must start with the character 4"
    exit()

## create random addresses until one of them matches the
desired prefix
## bruteforcing takes a while
while(1):
    rand_address = address.generate_random_address()
    if (rand_address[0:len(sys.argv[1])] == sys.argv[1]):
        print(rand_address)
        exit()
    else:
        print("searching")
```

7.4.4 Tutorial 4 - How to create a stealth address

The stealth address generation method explained in chapter 5 is somewhat complex, so a Python implementation is included here for assistance. Coding through a new process step-by-step can be very helpful for interpreting and internalizing the mathematics.

The goal of this tutorial is to generate a stealth address, using: a public view key, a public spend key, and a random private TX key (256-bit scalar).

First, the necessary dependencies are imported from the folder `libraries`

```
import os, sys
# library for hex
from binascii import hexlify, unhexlify
sys.path.append('../libraries')
# utils and ed25519 libraries
import utils
import ed25519
```

The `generate_stealth_address` function is defined, carrying out the necessary mathematical operations to create the unlinkable address from the public keys and some random information.

```python
def generate_stealth_address(publicViewKey, privateTxKey,
publicSpendKey, index):

## multiply r*A
derivation = utils.generate_key_derivation(publicViewKey,
privateTxKey)

## concatenate index to derivation then hash and reduce
## Hs(rA|i)
scalar = utils.derivation_to_scalar(derivation, index)

## multiply by base point
## Hs(rA|i)G
sG = ed25519.scalarmultbase(utils.hex2int(scalar))
## interpret the public spend key as a point on the curve
pubPoint  = ed25519.decodepoint(unhexlify(publicSpendKey))

## add the public spend key to the previously calculated
point
## Hs(rA|i)G + B
output = ed25519.edwards(pubPoint, sG)
## convert the point to a hex encoded public key
return hexlify(ed25519.encodepoint(output))
```

The code can be called like this:

```python
print(generate_stealth_address("be90718b250a06b4b-
cffca6af948240ad6d8951b730a9711f78d4c9decefb4bd",
"12b793b002ed168f36c9dc8d13c0e820546359452f67136f03087e-
b18208710e", "6b48d1c30a640b0b33d0062188df2edd4e6acac-
7282b215e86701a644a9f70ba", "01"))
```

Stealth addresses are not generated deterministically, since some random data is mixed in. An example output looks like:

```
a2bd788a63555e0847800b56051072d-
b3558ac2f97b58b8021e57c67125b4411
```

7.5 Monero C++ API

While interacting with Monero through the RPC interface is simple and easy to implement, it has its downsides. You can generate addresses and subaddresses, and even transfer funds. However, the RPC methods do not scale effectively, and could cause bottleneck issues for big enterprise applications.

Is there an alternative? Yes! Monero has a C++ API that can handle all functionality, including managing wallets and sending transactions.

The C++ API is a little trickier to use than the RPC interface, so you may not want to play around with it in a production setting, unless you're quite familiar with Monero integration. Any errors or problems along the way can break your security and privacy.

7.5.1 Monero libraries

The Monero Core is a collection of several simple libraries that are necessary or helpful for Monero activity - such as Boost, Ed2559, and the CryptoNight algorithm.

They are gathered to simplify common processes for developers; for example, a coder can simply call `base58_decode` from the Monero Core libraries instead of needing to manually create the function from scratch.

First you must compile libraries from the Monero Core. Once a library is compiled, an output file is created with a .a or .so extension.

7.5.2 Getting started with C++

To integrate the Monero Core code, you must first compile its libraries. Simply follow the instructions above, and check the dependecies table in chapter 6. Familiarity with C++ (specifically the basics for C++11 standard) will be very helpful for the following tutorial.

7.5.3 Tutorial 5 - Recovering all keys from the private spend key

This tutorial shows how to recover all Monero keys from the private spend key, making use of the C++ API and the CMake method. This tutorial is is intended for Linux-based platforms, since Apple and Windows have implemented their own libraries (for example, OpenSSL or Boost).

First, set all of the environment variables and libraries in a file named CMakeLists.txt. In this tutorial, we'll compile the Monero Core into /opt/monero folder.

```cmake
cmake_minimum_required(VERSION 3.5)

set(PROJECT_NAME tutorial-5)

project(${PROJECT_NAME})

set(CMAKE_CXX_FLAGS "${CMAKE_CXX_FLAGS} -std=c++11 -ldl")

if (NOT MONERO_DIR)
    # Path of Monero source code
    set(MONERO_DIR ~/monero)
endif()

message(STATUS MONERO_DIR ": ${MONERO_DIR}")

set(MONERO_SOURCE_DIR ${MONERO_DIR} CACHE PATH "Path to
the root directory for Monero")

# set location of Monero build tree
set(MONERO_BUILD_DIR ${MONERO_SOURCE_DIR}/build/Linux/
master/release/ CACHE PATH "Path to the build directory
for Monero")

set(MY_CMAKE_DIR "${CMAKE_CURRENT_LIST_DIR}/cmake" CACHE
PATH "The path to the cmake directory of the current proj-
ect")
list(APPEND CMAKE_MODULE_PATH "${MY_CMAKE_DIR}")

set(CMAKE_LIBRARY_PATH ${CMAKE_LIBRARY_PATH} "${MONERO_
BUILD_DIR}" CACHE PATH "Add Monero directory for library
searching")

# find boost
find_package(Boost COMPONENTS
        system
        filesystem
        thread
        date_time
        chrono
        regex
```

Continues on next page (1/3) »

```
        serialization
        program_options
        date_time
        REQUIRED)

# include boost headers
include_directories(
        ${Boost_INCLUDE_DIRS}
 )

include_directories(
            ${MONERO_SOURCE_DIR}/src
            ${MONERO_SOURCE_DIR}/external
            ${MONERO_SOURCE_DIR}/build
            ${MONERO_SOURCE_DIR}/external/easylogging++
            ${MONERO_SOURCE_DIR}/contrib/epee/include
            ${MONERO_SOURCE_DIR}/version
            ${MONERO_SOURCE_DIR}/external/db_drivers/
liblmdb)
# Specify source files
set(SOURCE_FILES main.cpp)

# Make executable
add_executable(${PROJECT_NAME} ${SOURCE_FILES})

set_target_properties(${PROJECT_NAME} PROPERTIES LINKER_
LANGUAGE CXX)

set(LIBRARIES
        wallet
        blockchain_db
        cryptonote_core
        cryptonote_protocol
        cryptonote_basic
        daemonizer
      cncrypto
        blocks
        lmdb
        ringct
        device
```

Continues on next page (2/4) »

```
        common
        mnemonics
        epee
        easylogging
        device
        pcsclite
        sodium
        ${Boost_LIBRARIES}
        pthread
        unbound
        crypto
        ringct_basic)

if (Xmr_CHECKPOINTS_LIBRARIES)
    set(LIBRARIES ${LIBRARIES} checkpoints)
endif()

set(LIBS common; blocks; cryptonote_basic; cryptonote_core;
cryptonote_protocol; daemonizer; mnemonics; epee; lmdb;
device; blockchain_db; ringct; wallet; cncrypto; easylog-
ging; version; checkpoints; ringct_basic; )

foreach (l ${LIBS})
        string(TOUPPER ${l} L)
        find_library(Xmr_${L}_LIBRARY
                     NAMES ${l}
                     PATHS ${CMAKE_LIBRARY_PATH}
                     PATH_SUFFIXES "/src/${l}" "/src/ringct"
"/src/" "/external/db_drivers/lib${l}" "/lib" "/src/crypto"
"/contrib/epee/src" "/external/easylogging++/"
                     NO_DEFAULT_PATH
                     )

        set(Xmr_${L}_LIBRARIES ${Xmr_${L}_LIBRARY})

        message(STATUS " Xmr_${L}_LIBRARIES ${Xmr_${L}_LI-
BRARY}")
        add_library(${l} STATIC IMPORTED)
set_
property(TARGET ${l} PROPERTY IMPORTED_LOCATION ${Xmr_${L}_
```

Continues on next page (3/4) »

```
LIBRARIES})
endforeach()
target_link_libraries(${PROJECT_NAME} ${LIBRARIES})
```

End (4/4)

Now that the libraries are added, it's time to develop our specific program. This derivation of all keys from the private spend key is a common task, necessary for generating or restoring wallets.

```cpp
// main.cpp file for Tutorial 5 - Mastering Monero
// https://github.com/monerobook/code/tutorial-5/main.cpp

#include "cryptonote_core/blockchain.h"
#include "common/base58.h"
#include "crypto/crypto-ops.h"
#include "crypto/hash.h"

// Converts crypto::hash into crypto::secret_key or cryp-
to::public_key
template <typename T>
T get_key_from_hash(crypto::hash & in_hash){
        T* key;
        key = reinterpret_cast<T*>(&in_hash);
        return *key;
}

int main(){
        // Put here your private spendable key!
        std::string str_spend_key = "f8f2fba1da00643bbf11f-
fec355a808d2d8ca4e4de14a10476e116abd8dd7f02";
        // Specify the network type. It could be cryp-
tonote::nettype, where nettype is MAINNET, TESTNET or
STAGENET
        cryptonote::network_type nettype = cryptonote::-
MAINNET;
        crypto::public_key public_spend_key;
```

Continues on next page (1/3) »

```cpp
    // Convert hex string to binary data
    cryptonote::blobdata blob;
    epee::string_tools::parse_hexstr_to_binbuff(str_
spend_key, blob);
    crypto::secret_key sc = *reinterpret_cast<const
crypto::
secret_key *>(blob.data());
    std::cout << "Private spend key : " << sc << st-
d::endl;

    // Generate public key based on the private key
    crypto::secret_key_to_public_key(sc, public_spend_
key);

    std::cout << "Public spend key : " << public_spend_
key  << std::endl;

    crypto::hash hash_of_private_spend_key;

    crypto::cn_fast_hash(&sc, sizeof(), hash_of_pri-
vate_spend_key);

    crypto::secret_key private_view_key;
    crypto::public_key public_view_key;

    // Generate keys from hash_of_private_spend_key
    crypto::generate_keys(public_view_key,private_view_
key,get_key_from_hash<crypto::secret_key>(hash_of_private_
spend_key), true);

    std::cout << "\n" << "Private view key : " << pri-
vate_view_key << std::endl;
    std::cout << "Public view key : " << public_view_key
<< std::endl;

    cryptonote::account_public_address address {pub-
lic_spend_key, public_view_key};
    std::string public_address;
    // Get account address as a string
    public_address = cryptonote::get_account_address_
```

Continues on next page (2/3) »

```
as_str(nettype, false, address);
        std::cout << "Monero Address:" << public_address <<
std::endl;
        return 0;
}
```

End (3/3) »

To compile the code, change to its directory and execute cmake. If you are in the root of the tutorial code repository, execute:

```
$ cd tutorial-5 && cmake .
```

The results should look similar to:

```
$ cd tutorial-5 && cmake .
-- The C compiler identification is GNU 6.3.0
-- The CXX compiler identification is GNU 6.3.0
-- Check for working C compiler: /usr/bin/cc
-- Check for working C compil-
er: /usr/bin/cc -- works
-- Detecting C compiler ABI info
-- Detecting C compiler ABI info - done
-- Detecting C compile features
-- Detecting C compile features - done
. . . . .

-- Configuring done
-- Generating done
-- Build files have been writ-
ten to: /code/tutorial-5
```

```
$ make
Scanning dependencies of target tutorial-5
[ 50%] Building CXX object CMake-
Files/tutorial-5.dir/main.cpp.o
[100%] Linking CXX executable tutorial-5
[100%] Built target tutorial-5
```

If you encounter any errors, please first verify that you have the correct version of CMake (>= v. 3.5.2) and GCC (>= v. 5). The CMake program will create a makefile for you, then we simply call the command:

Finally, launch the program by running `./tutorial-5`

```
Private spend key : <f8f2fba1da00643bbf11f-
fec355a808d2d8ca4e4de14a10476e116abd8dd7f02>
Public spend key : <fffb624bd31dfafb015b01c-
beaef28cbff3b2d77af01c54b77d6e1cef04d5f1e>
Private view key : <9227a05c665f684f5b8fef-
815cedd8a911b426c9fa07554c70daacf87757b302>
Public view key : <d79eaf3acfd1f7a93526d2eec-
5bec5b76b880177e2610b69716b4f0577950308>
Monero Address: 4BKjy1uVRTPiz4pHyaXXaw-
b82XpzLiowSDd8rEQJGqvN6AD6kWosLQ6VJX-
W9sghopxXgQSh1RTd54JdvvCRsXiF41xvfeW5
```

## Chapter 8

Wallet guide and troubleshooting tips

8.1 Specific instruction for Monero Official GUI

The following instructions show how to carry out the tasks described above through the Monero graphical user interface (GUI). If you are using a different wallet, you can skip this section.

1. Choose a language

The official Monero GUI can be downloaded from https://getmonero.org/downloads. Once you have unpackaged and launched the application, you will be presented with a language selection screen:

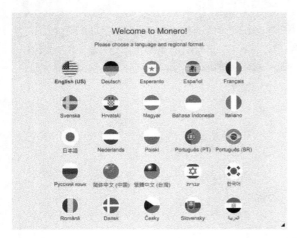

If you don't see your language above, please feel free to submit a translation to help others!

2. Specify an option

The Monero GUI offers three options for wallet type: Mainnet, Testnet, and Stagenet.

Choose Mainnet (default option) to access the regular blockchain with real Monero. The Testnet and Stagenet are two separate blockchains that are used by developers for developing and testing new code. The Testnet and Stagenet Monero do not have any real monetary value, and cannot be transferred to the mainnet.

If this is your first Monero wallet, press "create new wallet." The Monero software will generate a new seed for you, and show you the 25-word seed mnemonic.

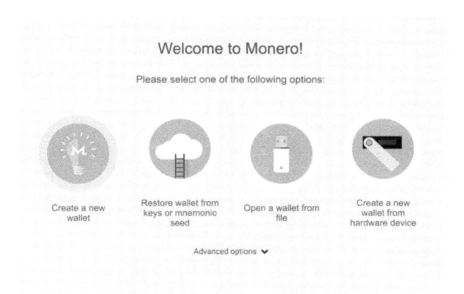

3. Write down the seed

Remember, the seed is not like a password! The network cannot restore access to your funds if you lose your seed.

Be sure to write this down and store it in a safe place where nobody else will find it!

4. Enter a password

You can enter a wallet password to keep your fund secure if somebody else accesses your computer. The wallet password is a local security feature, like a PIN screen unlock. It does not impact the cryptography or how your moneroj are stored on the blockchain, so restoring your wallet from the seed will bypass the local passphrase.

5. Download the Monero blockchain

Next, you will have the option to start your own node, or connect to a remote node.

Running your own node requires at least 60 GB of diskspace to store the blockchain. If your devices has limited resources, you can select "connect to a remote node" to configure a lightweight wallet that accesses data stored elsewhere. You can learn more about the pros and cons of using a remote node in section 4.2.3 "Local nodes" versus "remote nodes".

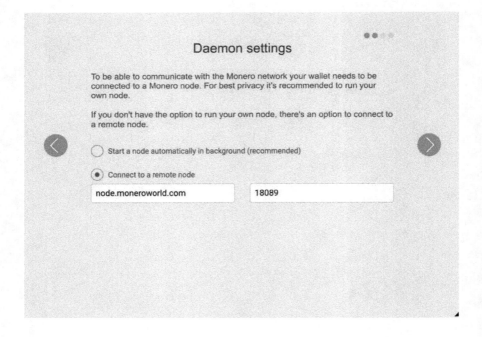

Then.. Welcome to Monero GUI!

8.1.2 Receiving Monero with the GUI

The "Receive" tab of the Monero GUI contains both the text and QR-code forms of your receiving addresses. The "Create new address" button generates more "subaddresses," which will all direct to this same wallet (seed). If you are charging somebody for a particular amount, you can enter the "Amount," which will then be encoded into the QR code.

8.1.3 Sending Monero with the GUI

To send Monero, you simply specify the amount that you wish to send, and the recipient's address. The Payment ID field can be left blank, unless your recipient specifies a Payment ID in advance. The Description field is stored locally, so you can leave notes for yourself. These will not be recovered if you restore your wallet from a seed.

Transaction History

8.1.4 Proof of Payment with the GUI

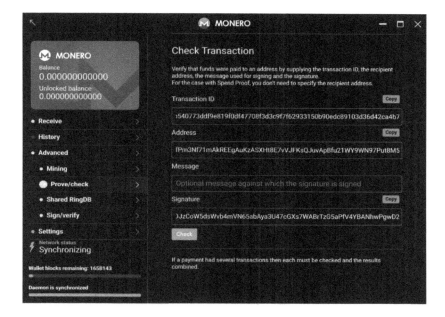

Proof of payment verification is available through the GUI under "prove/check." The screenshoot above shows the transaction ID, address, and transaction key from the Maria & Kahn example in chapter 2.

8.2 Specific instruction for Monero Wallet CLI

The following instructions show how to carry out the tasks described above through the Monero command line interface (CLI). If you are using a different wallet, you can skip this section.

8.2.1 Setting up a wallet with the CLI

The official Monero CLI can be downloaded from https://getmonero.

org/downloads. The command for running the CLI varies depending on your operating system. In Linux, simply launch `./monero-wallet-cli` from the program folder. You can add extra flags (documented in this Chapter) if you wish to connect to a remote node, bind your IP address, or other advanced options.

```
$ wget https://downloads.getmonero.org/cli/linux64

2014-08-12 (490 MB/s) - 'li-
nux64' saved [45719102/45719102]

$ tar jxvf linux64

./monero/
./monero/monero-wallet-rpc
./monero/monero-blockchain-import
./monero/monero-blockchain-ancestry
./monero/monero-blockchain-usage
./monero/monero-wallet-cli
./monero/monero-blockchain-depth
./monero/monero-gen-trusted-multisig
./monero/monerod
./monero/monero-blockchain-export
./monero/monero-blockchain-blackball

$ cd monero && ./monero-wallet-cli

2018-10-24 18:58:11,024 INFO  [de-
fault] Page size: 4096
This is the command line monero wallet. It needs
to connect to a monero daemon to work correctly.

WARNING: Do not reuse your Monero keys on anoth-
er fork, UNLESS this fork has key reuse mitiga-
tions built in. Doing so will harm your privacy.

Monero CODENAME (vX.X.X-release)

Specify wallet file name (e.g., MyWallet). If
the wallet doesn't exist, it will be created.
Wallet file name (or Ctrl-C to quit): (enter the
name of your wallet you want to create) testwallet
```

Continues on next page (1/3) »

```
No wallet found with that name. Confirm cre-
ation of new wallet named: testwallet
(Y/Yes/N/No): Yes
Generating new wallet...
Enter a new password for the wal-
let: (enter your secret password)
Confirm password: (confirm your password)
List of available languages for your wallet's seed:
0 : Deutsch
1 : English
2 : Español
3 : Français
4 : Italiano
5 : Nederlands
6 : Português
7 : русский язык
8 : Japanese
9 : Chinese
10 : Esperanto
11 : Lojban
Enter the number corresponding to the lan-
guage of your choice: (from 1 to 10)

Generated new wallet: 4BKjy1uVRTPiz4pHyaXX-
awb82XpzLiowSDd8rEQJGqvN6AD6kWosLQ6VJX-
W9sghopxXgQSh1RTd54JdvvCRsXiF41xvfeW5

View key: 9227a05c665f684f5b8fef815ced-
d8a911b426c9fa07554c70daacf87757b302
**********************************
***************************
Your wallet has been generated!
To start synchronizing with the dae-
mon, use the "refresh" command.
Use the "help" command to see the
list of available commands.
[...]

lamb hexagon aces acquire twang bluntly ar-
gue when unafraid awning academy nail threat-
en sailor palace selfish cadets click sickness
juggled border thumbs remedy ridges border
********************************
```

Continues on next page (2/3) »

```
* * * * * * * * * * * * * * * * * * * * * * * * * * * *
Starting refresh...
Background refresh thread started
[wallet 433bhJ]:
```

8.2.2 Receiving Monero

You can find out your address by typing address. If you wish to combine the address with a payment ID, you can type integrated_address to generate a random payment ID, or you can specify a particular ID as an input argument, such as:

```
[wallet 433bhJ]: integrated_ad-
dress 12346780abcdef00
```

You can review your incoming moneroj using the show_transfers command. Block height can be specified to list only recent transactions. For example, to only print transactions since block 650000:

```
[wallet 433bhJ]: show_transfers in 650000
```

8.2.3 Sending Monero

Use the transfer command to send Monero. To send moneroj to a single address, you do not have to specify the mixin number (during the October 2018, an hard fork requires to have a fixed mixin number of 11); you have to text the recipient address, and the amount to send.

194

To use the CLI to send the 0.6 XMR transaction describedabove, the command would be:

```
[wallet 433bhJ]:  transfer 4758W1dAkifB2G1wQK-
mPWRvPs9zdsb5ctRFW2ttQbkQxYHRuPRdHZ9ijq-
J7oxcns9SvtpiH8ti8BRjL3LUHaBURpiz4KF  0.06
```

8.2.4 Proof of payment

By default, transaction keys are not recorded by the CLI, however you can enable this by: `set store-tx-info 1`. You can locate a transaction key by specifying the transaction ID as the first argument of get_tx_key, for example:

```
[wallet 433bhJ]: get_tx_key
4b540773ddf9e819f0df47708f3d-
3c9f7f62933150b90edc8910 3d36d42ca4b7
```

To verify a transaction key, the syntax is: `check_tx_key TXID TXKEY ADDRESS`, so the command to check Maria's transaction key (from the chapter 2 example) would be:

```
[wallet 433bhJ]: check_tx_key
4b540773ddf9e819f0df47708f3d-
3c9f7f62933150b90edc891 03d36d42ca4b7
```

If you are looking far a payment that has a known payment ID, you can simply specify this in the `payments` command, e.g.

```
[wallet 433bhJ]: payments 12346780abcdef00
OutProofV1To53Qu2gegZbUevosKCTwrEdqiECgFyUygutXMEdh
```

8.3 Troubleshooting common problems

8.3.1 Problem: I transferred moneroj to my wallet, but my balance is still 0 XMR.

Available solutions:

1) [Always] Verify that you copied the correct Monero Address (sometimes malware can try to edit the copied Monero address);

2) Verify whether transaction actually arrived at your wallet / address by these steps:

A. Go to the Settings page of the GUI, and press on "Show seed & keys". Subsequently, copy the private view key.

B. Go to a blockchain explorer, such as xmrchain.net

C. Enter your transaction ID / hash.

D. Enter your private view key and address under "Decode outputs."

E. Click on decode outputs.

F. If the result shows "output true," it proves that the transaction was sent and recorded on the blockchain.

3) If step 2 above confirmed that the transaction occurred, then your moneroj are in the right place, but your wallet has not yet found the outputs. The Monero GUI uses a local cache that can take a few seconds to refresh, especially on Windows. If this problem persists, try to press the "Rescanning for outputs" on Monero GUI settings or try reach out through community channels for support (see chapter 6).

8.3.2 Problem: My GUI feels buggy / freezes all the time

First and foremost, it's important to make sure you're running the latest version. You can check the version number on the Settings page of the GUI (under Debug info). If you're not running the latest version, please upgrade first.

It is normal for the GUI to be less responsive during the initial sync process, during which the monerod daemon requires significant CPU resources to verify blocks and transactions.

You can limit monerod's CPU usage as follows:

1. Go to the Settings page of the GUI.
2. Add `--max-concurrency 1` to the "daemon startup flags" field.
3. Stop the daemon and exit the GUI.
4. Restart the GUI and daemon.

The restart is necessary to restart the daemon with the new `--max-concurrency` flag, which configures monerod to only utilize 1 CPU thread.

Glossary

Account

Accounts were created as part of the subaddress scheme. A wallet has a seed. From this seed, the primary address private spend and view keys are derived. From these private keys, subaddresses are derived. Subaddresses are grouped into accounts.

This primary address is the first address in the first account in the wallet.

Each account has its own balance, and can have multiple subaddresses associated with it. Since accounts are only groupings of subaddresses, there is no such thing as an account address (unless you count the first subaddress in the account as the "account address").

So a wallet can have multiple accounts, and each account can have multiple subaddresses.Since accounts and subaddresses are deterministically derived from the seed, you only need to know the seed in order to restore the account/subaddress structure when restoring a wallet (although any labels you assign to the accounts/ subaddresses will need to be noted separately).

Address

When you send Monero to someone you only need one piece of information, and that is their Monero address. A Monero Public address is a set of 95 characters starting with a '4'.

Airgap

An air gap, air wall or air gapping is a network security measure employed on one or more computers to ensure that a secure computer network is physically isolated from unsecured networks, such as the public Internet or an unsecured local area network.

The name arises from the technique of creating a network that is physically separated (with a conceptual air gap) from all other networks. The air gap may not be completely literal, as networks employing the use of dedicated cryptographic devices that can tunnel packets over untrusted networks while avoiding packet rate or size variation can be considered air gapped, as there is no ability for computers on opposite sides of the gap to communicate.

ASIC

An Application-Specific Integrated Circuit (ASIC) is an integrated circuit (IC) customized for a particular use, rather than intended for general-purpose use. For example, a chip designed to run in a digital voice recorder or a high-efficiency Bitcoin miner is an ASIC.

ASIC Resistance

ASIC resistance refers to measures taken by some cryptocurrencies to ensure that their mining algorithm is not compatible with this specialized equipment. See chapter 4, 5 and 6 to learn more about how the Monero community actively ensures that our CryptoNight algorithm is only accessible to CPU and GPU miners.

Base32 Address (Kovri)

A Base32 address is a shortened, encoded version of an I2P address. The Base32 address is the first part in a .b32.i2p hostname.

Bitmonero

BitMonero, previous name for the Monero Project, see chapter 1. Some legacy references are still included; for example, logs and the blockchain are stored in the ~/.bitmonero folder by default.

Block

A block is a container of transactions, with a new block being added to the blockchain once every 2 minutes on average.

Blocks also contain a special type of transaction, the coinbase transaction, which add newly created Monero to the network. Blocks are created through the process of mining, and the node that successfully mines the block then broadcasts it to each of the nodes connected to it, who subsequently re-broadcast the block until the entire Monero network has received it

Blockchain

A blockchain is a distributed database that continuously grows with a record of all of the transactions that have occurred with a given cryptocurrency. This database is often referred to as a ledger because the data contains a large list of transactions that have taken place.

In Monero, these transactions are packaged together into *blocks* every 2 minutes (on average), and all miners and nodes on the network have copies of these blocks.

Bulletproofs

Bulletproofs are a new mathematical system for verifiable masked transaction amounts. Bulletproofs shrinks transaction size by ~80%, and thus reduce fees dramatically.

Change

Monero sent as part of a transaction, that returns to your account instead of going to another recipient.

Coinbase Transaction

A special type of transaction included in each block, which contains a small amount of Monero sent to the miner as a reward for their mining work.

Command Line interface

A command line interface (or CLI) is a text-based interface used for entering commands via terminal. You can download the official Monero CLI (free and open source) at https://getmonero.org/downloads/

Consensus

Consensus describes a property of distributed networks like Monero where most of the participants follow the rules, and thus reject bad participants.

Cryptocurrency

A digital currency in which encryption techniques are used to regulate the generation of units of currency and verify the transfer of funds, usually operating independently of a central bank.

Cryptographic Signature

A cryptographic method for proving ownership of a piece of information, as well as proving that the information has not been modified after being signed.

Decoys

When constructing a Monero transaction, the term "decoy" refers to an output (not belonging to the spender) that is selected pseudo-randomly from the blockchain to serve as a mix-in for the ring signature. See section 5.4.3.

Denominations

A denomination is a proper description of a currency amount. it is oftentimes a sub-unit of the currency. For example, traditionally a cent is 1/100th of a particular unit of currency.

Monero denomination names add SI prefixes after dropping the initial "mo" for ease of use. The smallest unit of Monero is 1 piconero (0.000000000001 XMR). The plural amount for Monero is moneroj.

Name	Base 10	Amount
piconero	10^{-12}	0.000000000011
nanonero	10^{-9}	0.000000001
micronero	10^{-6}	0.000001
millinero	10^{-3}	0.001
centinero	10^{-2}	0.01
decinero	10^{-1}	0.1
MONERO	10^{0}	1
decanero	10^{1}	10
hectonero	10^{2}	100
kilonero	10^{3}	1,000
meganero	10^{6}	1,000,000

Difficulty

The difficulty is a network parameter that impacts how long it will take miners to find new blocks, by raising or lowering the bar for hash value that must be satisfied to complete a block. If more miners join the network, the difficulty increases to prevent blocks from being discovered too quickly (and the converse if network hash rate drops)

Encryption

In cryptography, encryption is the process of encoding messages or information in such a way that only authorized parties can decode and read what is sent. Encryption does not of itself prevent interception, but denies the message content to the interceptor.

Fees

Each transaction includes a fee that is collected by whichever miner includes the transaction in a completed block. Users with high-priority transactions can attach a relatively higher fee to incentivize miners to confirm the transaction sooner.

Fungibility

In economics, fungibility is the property of a good or a commodity whose individual units are essentially interchangeable. Cryptocurrencies with transparent ledgers lack this property, since each coin has a unique history, with its story recorded publicly. Monero achieves fungibility by combining several privacy technologies to prevent this deletrious information from being stored on the blockchain, thus rendering all moneroj indistinguishable.

Fluffy Blocks

A block is made up of a header and transactions. Fluffy Blocks only contain a header, a list of transaction indices, and any transactions that the node recieving the block may be missing. This saves bandwidth because nodes might already know about most or all of the transactions in the block and they don't need to be sent them again.

I2P

The I2P network provides strong privacy protections for communication over the Internet. Many activities that would risk your privacy on the public Internet can be conducted anonymously inside I2P.

Integrated address

An integrated address is an address combined with an encrypted 64-bit payment ID. A raw integrated address is 106 characters long.

Kovri

Kovri is a C++ implementation of the I2P network. Kovri is currently in heavy, active development and not yet integrated with Monero. When Kovri is integrated into your Monero node, your transactions will be more secure than ever before.

Mining

The process of cryptographically computing a mathematical proof for a block, containing a number of transactions, which is then added to the blockchain.

Mining is the distributed process of confirming transactions on the public ledger of all transactions, as known as blockchain. Monero nodes use the blockchain to distinguish legitimate transactions from attempts to re-spend coins that have already been spent elsewhere.

Monero is powered strictly by Proof of Work. It employs a mining algorithm that has the potential to be efficiently tasked to billions of existing devices (any modern x86 CPU and many GPUs). Monero uses the CryptoNight Proof of Work (PoW) algorithm, which is designed for use in ordinary CPUs and GPUs.

The smart mining feature allows transparent CPU mining on the user's computer, far from the de facto centralization of mining farms and pool mining, pursuing Satoshi Nakamoto's original vision of a true P2P currency.

Mnemonic Seed

A 13 or 25 word phrase used to backup a Monero account, available in a number of languages. This 25-word phrase (13 words in the case of MyMonero) has all the information needed to view and spend funds from a Monero account.

Monero

The most private cryptocurrency.

Node

A device on the internet running the Monero software, with a full copy of the Monero blockchain, actively assisting the Monero network.

OpenAlias

At its most basic, OpenAlias is a TXT DNS record on a FQDN (fully qualified domain name). The Monero Core Team released a standard called OpenAlias which permits much more human-readable addresses and "squares" the Zooko's triangle. OpenAlias can be used for any cryptocurrency and is already implemented in Monero.

Payment ID

Payment ID is an arbitrary and optional transaction attachment that consists of 32 bytes (64 hexadecimal characters) or 8 bytes (in the case of integrated addresses).

The Payment ID is usually used to identify transactions to merchants and exchanges: Given the intrinsic privacy features built into Monero, where a single public address is usually used for incoming transactions, the Payment ID is especially useful to tie incoming payments with user accounts.

Since the 0.9 Hydrogen Helix version, Payment IDs can be encrypted and embedded in a payment address called Integrated Address (in fact it's the integration between the payment ID and Monero Address). The Payment IDs of this type should be 64-bits and are encrypted with a random one-time key known only to the sender and receiver.

It is recommended to use the official wallet's integrated_address command to automatically generate Integrated Addresses that contain Compact Payment IDs. If you want to use the command line, you can generate Payment IDs as follows:

```
$ openssl rand -hex 8
```

Generating a Payment ID with 8 bytes

```
$ openssl rand -hex 32
```

Generating a Payment ID with 32 bytes

Pedersen Commitment

Pedersen commitments are cryptographic algorythms that allow a prover to commit to a certain value without revealing it or being able to change it.

When you spend Monero, the value of the inputs that you are spending and the value of the outputs you are sending are encrypted and opaque to everyone except the recipient of each of those outputs. Pedersen commitments allow you to send Monero without revealing the value of the transactions. Pedersen commitments also make it possible for people to verify that transactions on the blockchain are valid and not creating Monero out of thin air.

As long as the encrypted output amounts created, which include an output for the recipient and a change output back to the sender, and the unencrypted transaction fee is equal to the sum of the inputs that are being spent, it is a legitimate transaction and can be confirmed to not be creating Monero out of thin air.

Pedersen commitments mean that the sums can be verified as being equal, but the Monero value of each of the sums and the Monero value of the inputs and outputs individually are undeterminable. Pedersen commitments also mean that even the ratio of one input to another, or one output to another is undeterminable.

It is unclear which inputs are really being spent as the ring signature lists both the real inputs being spent and decoy inputs, therefore you don't actually know which input Pedersen commitments need to be summed. That's okay, because the ringCT ring signature only has to prove that for one combination of the inputs the outputs are equal to the sum of the inputs. For mathematical reasons, this is impossible to forge.

Ring Signatures

In cryptography, a ring signature is a type of digital signature that can be performed by any member of a group of users that each have keys. Therefore, a message signed with a ring signature is endorsed by someone in a particular group of people. One of the security properties of a ring signature is that it should be computationally infeasible to determine which of the group members' keys was used to produce the signature.

For instance, a ring signature could be used to provide an anonymous signature from "a high-ranking White House official", without revealing which official signed the message. Ring signatures are right for this application because the anonymity of a ring signature cannot be revoked, and because the group for a ring signature can be improvised (requires no prior setup).

A ring signature makes use of your account keys and a number of public keys (also known as outputs) pulled from the blockchain using a triangular distribution method. Over the course of time, past outputs could be used multiple times to form possible signer participants. In a *ring* of possible signers, all ring members are equal and valid. In Monero, ring signatures are used to conceal the sender of the reaction, by referencing several *possible* inputs for the transaction (including decoys).

Ring Size

Ring size refers to the total number of possible signers in a ring signature. If a ring size of 11 is selected for a given transaction, this means that there are 10 decoy outputs in addition to your "real" output.

Stealth Address

Stealth addresses are an important part of Monero's inherent privacy. They allow and require the sender to create random one-time addresses for every transaction on behalf of the recipient. The recipient can publish just one address, yet have all of his/her incoming payments go to unique addresses on the blockchain, where they cannot be linked back to either the recipient's published address or any other transactions' addresses. By using stealth addresses, only the sender and receiver can determine where a payment was sent.

Tail Emission

Monero block rewards will never drop to zero. Block rewards will gradually drop until tail emission commences at the end of May 2022. At this point, rewards will be fixed at 0.6 XMR per block.

Transactions

A cryptographically signed container that details the transfer of Monero to a recipient (or recipients).

The parameters of a transaction contain one or more recipient addresses with corresponding amounts of funds and a ring size parameter that specifies the number outputs bound to the transaction.

The more outputs that are used, a higher degree of obfuscation is possible, but that comes with a cost. Since a transaction gets larger with more outputs, the transaction fee will be higher.

It is possible to form a transaction offline, which offers additional privacy benefits.

A transaction can be uniquely identified with the use of an optional Transaction ID, which is usually represented by a 32-byte string (64 hexadecimal characters).

Wallet

A Monero account, or wallet, stores the information necessary to send and receive moneroj. In addition to sending and receiving, the Monero Wallet software keeps a private history of your transactions and allows you to cryptographically sign messages. It also includes Monero mining software and an address book.

Join the Monero community.
The doors are open, the fire is already lit,
and the people are welcoming.